I HEARD THE DONKEYS BRAY

I HEARD THE DONKEYS BRAY

Thirty Years in the Mission Field

by
Marguerite P. Boyce

Providence House Publishers
Franklin, Tennessee

Printed in the United States of America.

ISBN 1-881576-02-7

Published by
Providence House Publishers
Presbyterian Custom Publishing
P.O. Box 158, Franklin, Tennessee 37064.

For additional copies call 800-321-5692.

This book is dedicated with great appreciation and thanks to our children, who insisted we go back to school and learn to use a word processor, then had patience to coach us by telephone when we needed help. Also to our grandchildren David, Peter, Carolyn, Billy, Patricia and Neal, with a prayer that they will have the joy of following God's leading down life's hard roads.

Contents

Prologue

In 1940 the Board of World Missions of the Presbyterian Church, U.S. appointed James Reid and Marguerite Payne Boyce as Evangelistic and Educational Missionaries to Mexico. At that time, it was possible to obtain a permanent residence in Mexico by going to school six months of the year for five years. Without knowing any Spanish, James Reid enrolled in the summer session of the University of Mexico, taking three subjects: Mexican History, Mexican Literature, and the Conquest of Mexico. He passed these with good grades and learned Spanish.

When World War II broke out, the Mexican laws were changed and he was notified that he would have to attend the University as a full time student if he wanted to have residency status in Mexico. He must pass all subjects and be reaccepted at the end of each year. Also, he must be registered in the American Embassy Draft Board. (He had registered at the Embassy Draft Board on arriving in Mexico, so this was not a problem.)

After many hours of debate and prayer as to whether he should undertake such a long and tedious route in order to live in Mexico, permission was given for him to study medicine. He was asked to teach English in the Presbyterian Seminary in Mexico City and to help other missionaries with their paper work in obtaining Mexican official documents.

Medical school in Mexico requires seven years of academic work, including internship and a year of social service in a place approved by the National Department of Health.

The Mexico Mission and the Board of Missions in the United States wanted to open a new field in the State of Guerrero and build a hospital in a needy region. James Reid was asked to study, investigate, and survey the state during his last two years of Medical studies. Then he was to make a recommendation as to the best place to start the new work.

With this in mind, he asked the Mexican Health Department to allow him to spend his social service year in a small town on the upper coast of Guerrero. There he was appointed to study malaria in the village of Cacalutla, Guerrero. He finished the study and wrote his dissertation by November 1949. Then he applied for and was accepted for a Residency in Surgery at the Medical College of Virginia, to begin in July 1950. In the meantime, he and the Boyce family moved to Ometepec on the lower coast of the State of Guerrero, to survey this whole region. Having heard so many times that this was the most needy section of Guerrero, we felt we had to go see for ourselves.

The region had no roads but four wheel drive jeeps and trucks could make it over many of the donkey trails in dry season. In several of the larger towns, people had cleared fields so that airplanes could land, and soon there was a network of taxi planes which skipped over the mountains and landed in valleys or flat places dug out of a mountain side. Without knowing about trains or automobiles, the people were going from tediously slow travel by donkeys to flying like birds over the mountains. In the late 1940s a progressive pilot flew a DC-3 with cargo and mail into several villages and soon afterward the government added a few of the larger villages to their regular flights.

It would be more than twenty years before a paved road would be built over the rivers and mountains to reach the people in this region and before pick-up trucks would take over the work of donkeys.

For the remainder of this writing, I will refer to James Reid as "Jim," a name by which he has been known down through the years by many friends, associates, and family members.

Chapter I

We're Off

OMETEPEC, GUERRERO—1950

Early one morning in April Jim started the jeep and shouted "We're off." I looked around to be sure everyone was in place and safe. Jimmy, born just before Christmas in 1941, Florence, in March 1944, Peggi, in April 1947, were in their designated places and Elizabeth, born in July 1949, was happy in my lap in front. We left Tesquesquitengo where we had been waiting for months for official documents, and hoped we would reach Acapulco by dark. We had one more stop to make in Chilpancingo, the capital of the State of Guerrero, and I really dreaded that one.

"What will I do with the children while you go see Dr. Neri?" I asked anxiously. "It will be hot and everyone will be tired. Is there a restaurant or ANY place near the State Health Department Building where I could take them?"

"I can't remember," Jim replied, "But I don't think it will take long there. I only have to report and let him know we are actually going to Ometepec for a month."

He was optimistic, but I was not. "Won't take long" meant one thing to me and something entirely different in Mexico. But this time Jim was right. He had written ahead and told the doctor he would be there by noon and the secretary was expecting him. Dr. Neri was Director of Public Health for the State of Guerrero, and therefore was Jim's supervisor while we were living on the upper coast of Guerrero. When Jim had asked him where a hospital was most needed in the State, the doctor had hesitated then remarked "I can tell you where one is most needed, but you won't want to go there."

"I would certainly like to know," Jim replied, then added,

"Maybe I could visit it before going for my residency."

"It's definitely Ometepec," Dr. Neri said. "But there is no road there and the people have a terrible reputation. I would not like my family there."

His remarks had made Jim all the more determined to go see for himself. Ometepec had been mentioned by numerous people as being an isolated, neglected area where a hospital was most needed. Maybe the Lord was leading us that way.

Dr. Neri walked Jim back to the jeep and suddenly saw me and four other pairs of eyes looking at him. "You're not taking *them* are you?" he exclaimed, leaning down to see us better. He turned to me and said, "Senora, you are a brave woman."

"I don't know if I am brave or crazy," I replied, "but I am not brave enough to take that trip by land. Jim is going tomorrow in the jeep. The two oldest children will go with him and I shall leave the next day on the plane with the little ones."

We said good-byes and once more were on the way. It is good that God does not reveal the future to us as He guides us down life's road. If I had known at that point all that lay ahead, I doubt that I would have had enough faith to follow, and I would have missed one of the most rewarding twenty years a person could have.

As we had planned, Jim left the next morning at four o'clock. Jimmy and Florence were as quiet as mice as they jumped out of bed and dressed. Their food box had been packed the night before and it was only a few minutes until they were on their way.

The following morning I was at the airport early with Peggi and Elizabeth and several boxes of excess baggage. I eyed the DC-3 as it taxied up the runway and wondered if it really was air-worthy. This airline flew from Acapulco to Puebla with a number of short stops en route. Ometepec would be the third stop and would take about an hour. It was a cargo as well as passenger flight and, as we stood waiting, I assured Peggi that we were going to have a wonderful flight. In just one hour Daddy, Jimmy, and Florence would meet us in Ometepec.

The first two legs of the trip were easy, except for the take off at San Luis. This small town was located in a beautiful valley sur-rounded by high mountains. I was not at all sure we were going to clear the mountains, but suddenly we were out over the coastal plains once more. Fifteen minutes later we circled the Ometepec airstrip and I had my first view of the town.

April is the end of dry season so everything had a brown covering of dust. Some of the back patios had flowers that had been watered by their garden-loving owners. Then I saw the airstrip and my heart sank. Several teenage boys were wildly chasing cows and donkeys off the field so we had to circle again. I searched the road for the jeep, but the only vehicle was a truck. Several people were waiting for the plane, but my three were not among them.

We came to a sudden contact with dirt runway and bumped along to a stop. An old, rusty ladder was shoved and pulled to the door. The passengers casually began to debark.

"Cuidado" (careful) a pleasant looking man called to me, "Let me help you". He took my bags and helped Peggi down the steps, then pointing to the truck, told me to hurry and get in the cab before the plane took off.

I did not argue with him for I had seen the clouds of dirt and cow dung the plane had stirred up at the last two places. With a roar and the expected dust bomb, the plane took off and the owner of the truck piled the cargo into his truck. I had climbed out of the truck with Elizabeth, and Peggi came right behind me.

"Highway" to Ometepec—1950.

"Senor," I said, "my husband was supposed to meet me here and I am not sure where I am to go. All I have is the name of Dona Hermila."

"Don't worry," he assured me, "I know where you are to go. Your husband has not arrived in town yet but the pilot said he thought he saw a jeep coming up the last hill just out of town." With that, he helped Peggi back into the cab and held the door for me.

Senor Reyna, owner of the truck, was the agent for the airline. Besides selling tickets, he delivered cargo to and from the airport. He talked about the town on the way and told me it was just one week before the town would be crowded with merchants and people celebrating Easter week. Already they were building stalls on the side of the road. Dona Hermila lived on the Zocalo, (the town square) and we would be right in the thick of it all.

Dona Hermila came bustling out to greet me the moment we arrived and, in very fast Spanish, she welcomed me and told me she had saved us her very best two rooms and she knew our children would enjoy Ometepec at this time of year. I soon found out that all her rooms were "best rooms" and she had some reason for each of her renters to enjoy her hospitality.

I was not at all worried about where we would stay but was very anxious to know where Jim and the two children were. I was about to seek help when I heard a jeep and everyone informed me that it was my family arriving.

Main street was dirt with a few cobblestone terraces. It was definitely built for horses and donkeys and not for motorized vehicles, as Jim soon found out. I watched as he tried to hurry and realized everything in the trailer and the people in the jeep were receiving a terrible shaking.

Everything, including the humans, was covered with dust.

"We had fun," Jimmy exclaimed. "We spent the night in a man's back yard and saw all the stars."

"And he had a baby deer," Florence added.

"We'll tell Mommy all about it after we unload things." Jim said. Then, telling some of the boys he would pay them to help, we settled in for our Ometepec adventure.

We had two large rooms and one end of the porch. The rooms were across the porch from each other and one jutted out into the back patio, a common yard for all renters of the house. Our bedroom was on the street side and it didn't take long for us to realize we would have to close the large wooden windows if we were to have any privacy. We had indeed caused quite an excitement in town and only the bars over the window kept the village children from pouring into our quarters. Our children on the inside were just as curious about the ones on the outside. The baby's playpen was the first thing I wanted unpacked and she was as happy to be out of my arms as I was to put her down. "Look," one of the children in the window shouted, "The baby has a box!"

"That's not a box," another one replied, "it's a baby corral. Look at that, they put their baby in a corral."

Jimmy helped put up the army cots we were to call beds for this month, and Florence and I started on the kitchen. The butane gas stove we brought was the first one in town and as soon as it was connected I began preparing some lunch. The landlady saw the stove and immediately called all the women cooking in the yard to come see this stove that did not make smoke. The commotion that followed made me wonder if I would survive a whole month in this place. Screams of excitement brought other women and all wanted to know if all Americans cooked on this blue fire. One young girl came to look, then called to her mother in the street, "Come look at this stove that just burns air. If we bought one of these we wouldn't have to go gather wood every day."

Then the stream of women and children came by selling tortillas and fruit. I decided to forget the cooking and opened a jar of peanut butter (a true delicacy in Mexico). Spreading it on hot tortillas, I gave the children one of their favorite lunches. Before two hours had passed, we had pineapples, papayas, bananas, and persimmons added to our regular diet.

By night time, we were all exhausted. I had bathed the two smallest children at the common wash place in the yard. This was a cement tank about four feet square and five feet deep that held the water for the entire household. Dishes, clothes, and small children were placed on a cement washboard built onto the side of the water supply. Water was scooped out of the tank with gourds and poured over whatever was being washed. The rest of us bathed in the bedroom by candle light. I had packed my

oblong tin tub with towels, sheets, and clothes for I was determined we would not bathe in the communal baths I had seen in
other small towns.

Finally, everyone was clean and well-fed and the street began
to calm down. I read a story to the children and soon we were all
asleep.

Suddenly, there was a loud noise and a loudspeaker began to
announce that bingo was being played in the street by the town
square. The barker could be heard all over town and as our
rooms were directly on the town square, I thought for a moment
we were being invaded. Loud country music followed the
announcement. As soon as the music stopped, the announcement
was made again, imploring everyone to come enjoy this wonderful game. More music, another invitation, and after a half hour of
announcing that they were going to have a bingo game, the fun
started. The generator furnished the two light bulbs for the game
but many people had their own candles. Our children did not
even awaken, and Jim even slept after the first hour. However. I
listened to them call numbers and shout when someone won a
game until they stopped playing at midnight.

At six a.m., the street came alive with vendors, children and
donkeys. Someone had a charcoal cooker just outside our window and the smell of tortillas and beans filled our room.

"Man, am I hungry," came from Jimmy's corner of the room.
"Me, too," chimed in Florence and Peggi. So we were up to start
the day as the first rays of light came over the mountain.

In less than twenty-four hours, we learned that Dona Hermila was not only the town gossip, she was equal to a town crier and
newspaper. Jimmy and I went to the market to buy some meat
and were bombarded with questions. Is it true your husband is a
doctor? Are you going to stay here? Do you have medicine for
malaria?

Before we returned home, Jim had already had his first call to
see a sick child. A blind man, who played a guitar and sang for a
living, lived nearby and one of his children was very ill with
fever and diarrhea. Wouldn't the doctor please come quickly to
see him?

I took the children in the kitchen for breakfast and Jim left
with the boy who had brought the message. Without realizing it,

Blind singer being led to market by his son.

we had started what was to be our typical schedule for many years. Regular meals were usually without Daddy at the table, but snacks were had whenever Daddy rushed in to eat.

Elizabeth's swing seat had been secured over a rafter in the ceiling, so now she had two places to be a part of the activity. She could bounce up and down in the middle of the kitchen or be in her playpen in the other room. She loved the kitchen spot and soon learned to squeal if she wanted a push from someone passing by. One woman who brought tortillas called Elizabeth, "The little white dove in her nest."

I had forgotten about the doctor in Chilpancingo saying that the people in this region were bad until about a week later. I looked up to see a stranger hiding behind a door. I was glad Jim was at home, and was about to call him, when the man motioned for me to be quiet. I realized then that the man was more frightened than I was, so I left him there and stepped back into the bedroom to tell Jim.

"Yes, I know who he is," Jim said,"He told me last night that someone was looking for him to kill him. He rented the last room at the corner of the side street and hasn't been outside in several days. Hermila told him some men had asked her if he had rented a room and she had said, "No." But the man was afraid they had seen him when he arrived so had not left the house. This morning someone had banged on the back yard door while he was in the bath house. He was afraid the gunmen had invaded his room, so had hurried into our corner of the porch to hide.

Before I could decide what to say to the children, Dona Hermila came hurrying through the yard. She knew the man was hiding behind the door to our kitchen for she had sent him there. She had also personally checked his room and the back patio and assured all of us it was safe for him to return to his quarters. The man told us he was leaving that morning and would not bother us again. He apologized for frightening me and then slipped through the yard without another word.

By Palm Sunday, the town was alive with vendors and buyers. This week was the traditional fiesta week of the whole year. People came from as far as Toluca, more than two days travel away (west of Mexico City) to sell handwoven blankets and shawls. The "Reboso", or long light-weight shawl that even the poor women must own, was on sale everywhere and prices and quality were compared with great diligence. Men examined the machetes, knives and all types of horse saddles and equipment. Streets were blocked off and each merchant's stall was covered with either leaves or palm branches or bright colored pieces of cheap cloth.

I was informed by my neighbor that I would need three new dresses. One for Thursday, one for Friday, and one for the big celebration on Friday night. I was curious about Easter Sunday and asked what they did on that day.

"Oh, Semana Santa is over on Friday. By Sunday everyone has packed up and is trying to get back home."

Our children enjoyed the holiday atmosphere and because we lived on the main square, they had as much fun watching the locals, as the locals did watching these children with completely different looks. I decided while living in Mexico City that our children were a great asset. Mexicans love children and would often stop us to ask about feeding and caring for our family.

The blind man's son, who had been so sick when we first came, was getting well. After leading his father to his bench in the market, he would come sit in the street just below our window. He and Jimmy talked about everything that happened.

He explained many of the local customs to our children as

they watched and listened to him through the bars.

On Monday of Holy week, a man in civilian clothes knocked on our door and greeted my husband with, "Dr. Boyce, I am Father Chey, the priest in a village in the mountains. I heard that an American doctor was in Ometepec for our fiesta and I would like to talk with you."

"Oh, yes," Jim exclaimed. "I am honored. Please come sit at our table and have some coffee."

I was introduced and each of the children, in good Mexican style, repeated his or her name and shook hands. They then went to watch the activities going on in the street so that the two men could have a long talk. After serving coffee and cookies, I too, with Elizabeth, went to get a bucket of water at the tank in the middle of the yard. The wife of the army captain, who lived in another apartment in the complex, came rushing to see me.

"Did I see Father Chey go in to see the doctor?" she asked. "Yes," I replied, "Do you know him?"

She certainly did and was more than anxious to tell me about him. He was born and raised in Ometepec but his family had given him to the church when he was a boy and he had gone to Puebla to study when he was fourteen years old. He had asked to be sent back to the coastal region when he was ordained and had lived in a number of towns up and down the State of Guerrero.

"Some of the towns had run him out because of bad conduct. And he is not in good standing with the Bishop in our Cathedral," she warned me, "So be careful what business you have with him.

Having delivered her gossip and let me know she did not like Father Chey at all, she returned to her house. I had already been made aware of her dislike for foreigners and especially those who were not of her religion.

After the priest left, Jim told me what he had learned. Father Chey had not wanted to be a priest but had always wanted to be a doctor. He was heart-broken when his family insisted that he dedicate his life to the Church. When he returned to the coastal region, his greatest desire was to help the people improve their living conditions. Malaria, typhoid and intestinal parasites take their toll every year.

"Your surgical residency would be of great value in this region. With a hospital and the facilities to do surgery, great advances in medical treatment could be accomplished. Other young doctors would not look at this region as hopeless."

"I understand," Jim had replied. "I asked many of my classmates about coming here, and not one would come to this region. They all think it is over loaded with bandits."

"If you will come here, you will be welcome," the Father said. "The religous fanatics will try to scare you off, but do not be afraid. Come back right here after your year of surgical residency and I will take you out to my villages and show you around the entire region. You are needed here. I shall be waiting for you."

April is one of the hottest months of the year and, because it is the very end of the dry season, it is dusty. People who live in the houses along the main street must sweep their street and sprinkle water on it every morning. Usually the elderly or young boys have this chore. Dona Hermila had an old man come before daylight every morning to sweep the street and yard and, as water became scarce, we were asked to save bath water to sprinkle the street. Pigs were allowed to roam freely through the town and they were the only garbage collectors we saw. There were no public toilets, so the back streets were used. At times the stench was so bad the home owners complained to the town officials. Fortunately, the sun was hot and the streets were baked by noon.

Flies were my greatest enemy. Flies during the day and large roaches at night. When Jim had bought the army jeep trailer, we were given the mosquito netting sides to an army tent. These we had put around the kitchen and, although they didn't keep out all the flies, they did help.

Roaches were another matter. These I fought the entire time we lived in Ometepec and I must admit they won. They came in all sizes and all shades of brown. From tiny light brown ones to huge thick-backed black ones, they crawled across the floor at night. Scorpions also came out at night and all of us learned to keep shoes by our beds, but always to shake them out before putting a foot inside.

The one local custom I truly loved was the afternoon "Siesta", that wonderful time of day when it was too hot to do anything but be quiet and rest. Even the donkeys and dogs found shade where they could nap. Stores were closed from one o'clock until three. Everyone ate dinner and rested. For many, this was the only meal of the day. At other times, it was eat whatever you could find to eat. Only the rich sat at a table to eat and only the very rich had tableware. Indians carried bowls made of gourds. These were placed inverted on their heads when walking, but used as cups for drinking or as dishes for any kind of food. Tortillas were broken into bite sizes and used as spoons for eating.

On Monday of Easter week, about two o'clock in the afternoon, a guitar was strummed just outside our window and a popular Mexican song sung in a beautiful tenor voice. Then a love song, followed by another popular country western. I knew I would never get to sleep, so I began to listen to the words and the beautiful but untrained voice. Jim leaned over me and whispered, "It's the blind man serenading us because his little boy is well. I would not let him pay me anything for the medicine I gave him so he said he would serenade me this week."

True to his word, he came every day at two o'clock and sang. The first day, I said a prayer for him and his family and added: "Lord, I'd rather listen to this man than the bingo players, so please let me sleep tonight, so I can make it through tomorrow."

By Thursday, the town was swarming with so many people the donkeys and horses had to be left outside the city limits. Three days had been spent comparing prices and quality and now the bargaining began. The noise level grew higher and higher as the hours passed. One merchant would try to shout louder than the others. Friends who saw each other only at these fiestas would greet each other with the typical hugs and handshakes and exchange news of families and friends.

As darkness came, the bingo games began and the noise reached its highest peak. Suddenly, two shots rang out and women screamed for their children to run. We were in our kitchen, just beginning our meal, when the army captain on the other side of the house came running in.

"They've killed Don Sabino," he announced so everyone could hear. "Don't go into the street. They were after German Miller, but he was in the back patio. Don Sabino had answered the knock at the door and the killer thought he was Don German."

Senor Miller was a rich merchant of German-Mexican heritage. His grandfather had migrated to Mexico after the first

World War and settled in Ometepec. He was a cattle rancher and, because he could out-wit others, he made many enemies.

The town was quiet for about an hour as the army tried to find the murderer. Suddenly, the bingo started again and people soon filled the streets. They did not catch the attacker and everyone declared he was a paid killer as he did not recognize Don Sabino. Anyone from the region would have known Don German.

Friday night there was a Mass at the cathedral, then the party began again. Merchants began packing up their wares about ten o'clock and by Saturday morning early they were on their way to another town for Sunday market.

"What about Easter morning?" I asked Dona Hermila, "don't you have any kind of service for the resurrection?"

"No," she replied with a puzzled look, "Friday night Mass is the last of the celebration. The party afterward is because Lent is over and now we can have weddings and other celebrations."

On Sunday morning, we had our little Easter service and the children colored pictures of the empty tomb. The town was very quiet and once again we heard the donkeys braying as they came home down the main street.

A week later we, too, prepared to leave. Many people came by to bid us good-bye and tell us to come back after Jim finished his residency. Dona Hermila came in one afternoon and, walking over to my stove, proclaimed, "This stove is not leaving Ometepec. I will buy it from you, or take it from you, but you must not take it out of here. You can buy another, but I would never be able to get one brought in without being charged an enormous amount of money."

"How will you get gas when this tank gives out?" I asked.

"That is not a problem. Trucks will be going out for another month and they can find the tanks in Acapulco. It's the stove they are afraid will be damaged in hauling. Think it over, for I know two other women who want to buy your stove and anything else you want to sell. Just remember, I told you first."

Jim was delighted when I told him. He had thought about selling many of the things. He had experienced a rough time twice on the trip in and had to make several attempts before reaching the top of one steep hill. He had Jimmy and Florence walk up to the top and wait for him. They cheered him on as he struggled to reach the highest point. Three times he had had to back down the hill and get another running start to pull up the ungraded road.

The stove and two tanks of gas were the heaviest luxuries we had, and he would be glad to sell them, and anything else anyone wanted. He was very anxious to lighten the load going back.

Mail finally arrived three days after the week of holidays, and among other much-welcomed letters was one from a friend in Teloloapan. Jack had arranged to leave his Agriculture station and come to help Jim drive out to Acapulco. He would arrive two days before our departure date in order to help pack up and load the jeep and trailer. I said a prayer of thanksgiving for good friends and bought tickets on the plane for the children and me.

A week later we were on our way back to the U.S.A. and the year of surgical residency at the Medical College of Virginia in Richmond. We had stayed well during our sojourn in Ometepec and I gave thanks to our loving, Heavenly Father who looked after us.

O Master let me walk with Thee
In lowly paths of service free;
Tell me Thy secret; help me bear
The strain of toil, the fret of care.

O Master Let Me Walk with Thee
Washington Gladden, 1879

Chapter II

Tears, Prayers, Hope

Jim finished his year of surgical residency, Jimmy did well in third grade, Florence also did well in first grade, and Peggi, Elizabeth, and I had enjoyed our rather quiet home. We had traveled many miles speaking to churches about the possibilities in southwest Mexico and the dire need for both secular and Christian education. So by late June 1951, the time had come for us to leave Richmond and return to Mexico.

In Dallas, Texas, with the help of Dr. Tom Currie, the Minister of the Oak Cliff Church, we exchanged our old Ford for a Chevrolet suburban carry-all with large tires so that travel over muddy roads might be easier. One of our supporting churches collected medicines and medical instruments, and we felt truly prepared for anything the future might bring.

By the time we had returned to Mexico, the rains had started, and everyone said we would have to wait until dry season to reach Ometepec. Also the Mission Board in the U.S.A. had said they did not want just one family to go into such an isolated, desolate territory. We would have to find another family to go with us.

John and Madge Wood had joined the Mission in 1949 and had studied Spanish in Zitacuaro for a year. They were going to another small town in the State of Guerrero for a year, then would be ready to look at Ometepec. In the meantime, Jim was asked to go to Morelia, Michoacan to help in the hospital there until we could get to Ometepec.

Morelia proved to be the most agonizing misfortune of our life in Mexico. We rented a nice house in a good neighborhood and settled rapidly into our routine of school and mission life.

The first month was easy except for the flies. The General who lived behind us had some very fine pigs which he kept against the wall in his back patio. The pigs didn't bother us but the flies from the pig pen bothered the entire neighborhood. We found someone to screen the windows but it took over a month to complete the job.

One August Sunday morning Jimmy didn't want any breakfast and said he didn't want to go to church. Florence said her head hurt and she didn't want to go either. I took their temperatures and called Jim at the hospital where he was making morning rounds.

"Jimmy and Florence both have fever," I said. "Please bring some medicine for them."

"Any other symptoms?" he asked.

"Well, Florence says her head hurts, and Peggi just said her stomach hurts. Please come as soon as you can."

He walked in the door a few minutes later just as Peggi vomited her breakfast. I had put Jimmy and Florence to bed and picked up Elizabeth, who by that time was also showing signs of feeling bad.

"You shouldn't pick her up," Jim said in a disapproving voice. I was five months pregnant and had been having back pains for several weeks.

"I know it," I snapped. "She's very hot and I believe she has fever also. What do you suppose has hit all of them at the same time?"

While he was examining Jimmy, Elizabeth sent her breakfast all down my dress and Florence rushed into the bathroom but missed the basin.

The next twenty-four hours were a nightmare. Early Monday morning, Jim said he had to help with an operation at the hospital and wanted to talk with Dr. Ross and maybe call Dr. Rodriguez in Mexico City. Dr. Ross was the other missionary on the staff and Director of the hospital. Dr. Rodriguez was a fine Mexican pediatrician, a graduate of Tulane Medical School and had post-graduate training at Mayo Clinic.

Jim came home before noon and I could tell by the expression on his face that he was worried. He went to check on the children immediately and was glad to find the fever down for the two younger ones, but still rather high for Jimmy and Florence.

"You go lie down and get some rest," he said to me. "I'll watch them for an hour or two. Dr. Ross said he would cover for me this afternoon and I don't have to go back. I have some new medicine Dr. Rodriguez recommended that I'll give the kids. Go rest, for we have to watch them carefully tonight."

"What do they think it is?" I asked again.

"We don't know yet. I'll tell you when I know."

I went to lie down for I was tired and knew the night would be long. I could tell by the look on Jim's face that he was worried and I sensed that he didn't want to tell me what ailment he suspected the children had.

We took turns sitting up that night and only slept in short naps. It was not very satisfying sleep but the body someway managed to keep going. About two o'clock in the morning I was awakened by the sound of Jim agonizing in prayer.

"What's the matter," I said as I sat up in bed. He climbed into bed, put his arms around me and said between sobs, "Florence asked me for a sip of Pepsi and I gave it to her. She took one swallow, then choked. I thought she would never breathe again. She turned blue and I cried out to God, 'Help! Save her! Help me...' and suddenly she started to breathe again. I have been sitting by her bed for the last hour and she seems all right now. But Honey," he cried with tears running down his face, "I'm afraid the children have polio."

Between trips to check on each child, we prayed for wisdom and guidance. We questioned our plans for the future and wondered what we should do. Where should we go? Surely the Lord had not brought us this far then closed the door.

The next day Dr. Ross came to see the children and he had talked to Dr. Rodriguez in Mexico City. Both of them advised us to wait until the children had no fever and then take them to Mexico City, where the American Polio Foundation was just opening up a polio ward at the British-American Hospital and we could see what was offered there. That would be our first step. In the meantime, I was to keep the children quiet. A new children's dosage of aspirin and phenobarbitol was on the market and the two youngest could take that.

Days were filled with keeping the children quiet, preparing

food they could eat, (especially for Florence as she continued to have trouble swallowing) and keeping the medicine dosage correct for each child and giving it on time. We tried to keep cheerful and we read books over and over.

Nights were filled with crying, or being too tired to cry; with praying for guidance and wisdom, and asking over and over, what shall we do, where shall we go? Shall we leave Mexico?

The first night we had given the aspirin with phenobarbitol to Peggi and Elizabeth, I sat reading children's books until they went to sleep. Peggi was asleep in a few minutes but Elizabeth, instead of sleeping, began to sing. Then she jumped up on the bed and began to dance and sing.

"Elizabeth," I pleaded, "Please lie down. The Doctor said for you to be quiet." I took her in my arms and tried to rock her but my lap was too small by now and she wanted to clap her hands and dance. We found out that night that phenobarbatol had the opposite effect on Elizabeth than it had on the other children, so Jim and I took turns watching as she worked off her "high."

I began packing clothes and separating what we would take to Mexico City or leave behind in Morelia. As I began to put their toys in the closet under the stairway, I suddenly began to cry. "Oh God, what am I supposed to do with these things? It takes two legs to ride a bike and two feet to skate. Jimmy has one leg and one arm paralyzed. Oh, what are we supposed to do?" I made fists and began to beat on the boxes I had just packed away. I don't know how long I was there beating the boxes and crying, but when I finally wiped my eyes and came out, I was tired yet felt I could once again face the problems before us. Somehow, I knew our loving God had not been angry with me for beating the boxes and crying, for in my heart I felt He understood. And I knew that somehow He would guide us to do the right thing for our children. They were His children, too, for we had given each one to Him as infants. They were children of the covenant.

A week later we loaded the carry-all again. The two back seats were removed and a platform was made the size of a mattress. Suitcases and boxes were packed under the platform and the mattress was made into a bed. Peggi and Elizabeth did not have any paralysis and had plenty of room to sit up. Jimmy and Florence thought it fun to have a bed to ride on.

Just before leaving we received a telegram from friends in Columbus, Georgia. "Process started for children to enter Warm Springs. Advise us condition of children and possible arrival time."

As we drove back over the beautiful mountain ranges to Mexico City, I thought of the hymn, "My Jesus as Thou Wilt." Now the second verse kept ringing in my heart:

> My Jesus as Thou Wilt,
> Though seen through many a tear,
> Let not my star of hope
> Grow dim or disappear.

We arrived in Mexico City in late afternoon and went directly to the hospital. Dr. Rodriguez had already notified them that we would arrive late and that the children should be admitted to the new unit for polio patients. The next morning he would see the two younger children at his office. The physiotherapist was an American and had been sent to Mexico by the Polio Foundation. She had been well trained in Warm Springs, Ga., and was so cheerful and kind the children immediately liked her.

As we were about to leave the hospital, we received a message that helped us decide to remain in Mexico City. A couple working with the Wycliffe Bible Translators was leaving for a six months' furlough in a day or two and offered us their house while they were away. Surely God was working things out for us.

Dr. Rodriguez could find no paralysis in Peggi or Elizabeth but said they should not get too tired and should take rest periods twice a day for several weeks. Otherwise, they could have a normal active life.

I went to see our good friend Dr. Marroquin, the obstetrician who had delivered both Peggi and Elizabeth. I was declared in good health considering the fact that I had not paid attention to my diet or medicine for the last several weeks. The baby I was carrying seemed fine and was certainly active enough.

Dr. Marroquin had heard about the children and our dilemma as to whether we should go to Warm Springs or stay in Mexico. He assured us again that the new unit for polio in the British-American Hospital was one of the most modern, with fine equipment and a very fine physiotherapist. "You will probably get more personal attention here as they are not so crowded and are training some of our finest nurses in modern therapy."

The house offered to us was a small but adequate three bedroom, Mexican-style house with a walled-in back patio and a closed-in car port in front. Those dear friends had left the house well furnished and all we had to do was to move in and settle down. With Jimmy and Florence in good hands in the hospital and the two younger children tired enough to fall asleep as soon as put to bed, Jim and I had our first good night's sleep in weeks. Prayers of thanksgiving poured from our hearts that night. We especially gave thanks for our Christian friends and the network of love we had encountered on all sides.

At our Mission meeting in late January of 1952, it was voted that the Boyce and Wood families move to Ometepec for a one year trial. If, by the end of the rainy season of 1953, we felt Ometepec was not the place for a new hospital, or too dangerous for our families, we were to leave during the dry season. Jim and Johnny were to go to Ometepec as soon as they could to try to rent houses and make them livable in time to truck in our furniture before the rains made it impossible to move.

Doctors had released Florence from the hospital at Christmas 1951, and said Jimmy could leave by May. He was improving rapidly and especially enjoyed swimming in the warm pool. All the children were excited about going to Ometepec again.

During our mission meeting we discovered that both Johnny and Madge were very musical. Johnny was the only bass in our group and Madge had a very good soprano voice. Jim was a tenor and I could sing in the alto range. We began singing quartets any time we were together and made it a joyous occasion for the fourteen years we worked together.

Madge was expecting their third child, due five weeks after our fifth. They rented a small apartment near our rented house, and we began making plans for our move. Johnny and Jim made one trip down by plane to look over Ometepec. Many people recognized Jim and urged him to hurry back. The two men rented a room with Dona Hermila and walked all over town looking for houses for rent. Then, just about the time for them to fly back to Mexico City, one of the prominent men in town came to visit them.

"We've been told not to rent to you two because you are

foreigners and Protestants. But I'm not afraid of you nor the others. I have a house that I will rent to you and my widowed sister-in-law has one just a block from mine that she will rent to the other one of you. If you would like, I'll take you there right now to show you. They both need some repairs which we can take out of the rent if you do them, or we can charge higher rent and we can hire it done."

The two men certainly wanted to see the houses and set out immediately with the man to see what were to be our future homes. One thing we learned early about Johnny Wood was that he was an optimist and always anxious to get started on whatever he felt necessary to take the next step. Jim was also an optimist though a more cautious one. At this point, both men felt this man had been inspired by God to rent them houses, and they were jubilant when they returned to Mexico City. They had been sent to rent houses and that they had done. Also they had looked at both houses and had decided what work would be needed.

One house had three very large rooms and needed fewer repairs than the other. We would be ready to go in May, therefore they had designated that house as the Boyce residence. Madge would not be ready to leave the City until the last of May, so Johnny would have an extra month to work on their house.

I was always the one with the difficult questions and I'm sure I must have asked the questions Jim dreaded to hear. "What about the kitchen? What kind of bath and toilet accommodations are there? Is there water available in the house or do we have to have it carried in?"

"Give me time to answer one question at a time," Jim interrupted me. "There is a spigot of water in the back yard. We can make a connection into the house. We plan to add a porch the length of the house and make a kitchen at one end and a bathroom at the other end. In between will be your school room and a work space. The middle room is big enough to divide into three rooms. We can fix it up to be all right for just one year. Then if we stay in Ometepec we will build to our own plans."

"We're lucky, too," Johnny said, We have a whole wash stand in the yard and we will also connect water to kitchen and bath room when we get the bathroom built."

The two men worked late into the night planning what to

take with them. They would each drive a jeep and trailer and take as many necessities as they could manage. Furniture would be shipped via cargo trucks. Everything would have to be in Ometepec by the end of May when the rains started.

My days were filled with teaching Florence second grade by use of a correspondence school, then going to the hospital in the afternoon to help Jimmy with fourth grade. Jimmy was now getting around in a wheel chair that was equipped with a sling for his right arm. He could not write as his arm and hand were still partially paralyzed. I had worried that I would have to teach him to write with his left hand, but both the school and the doctor said to wait awhile. In the meantime, I wrote for Jimmy as he dictated his math, spelling and other questions. On weekends he was allowed to come home and we relaxed and planned things we would do in Ometepec.

Jim decided he'd better remain in Mexico City until the baby arrived but he and Johnny were scouting the town daily for materials they would need. Neither man had ever done very much building, and Madge and I wondered what we would find when we arrived. Jim had worked one summer as a plumber's assistant and knew how to connect two pipes. Madge was an artist and drew plans for both houses and helped them estimate the amount of pipe and other supplies to buy.

The morning of Monday, February 25, we were to take Jimmy back to the British-American hospital and Florence was to go for physical therapy. On the way to the hospital, I remarked to Jim that I thought I should be left at Dr. Marroquin's hospital after we delivered the two children. I was large enough to have twins and was very uncomfortable.

We promised Florence that Daddy would be back in about an hour and left her and Jimmy in care of an orderly at the door. Then we hurried through early morning traffic to the small private hospital where Elizabeth had been born. Jim was anxious to take the two younger children back home so he called Madge to see if she could go over with her two boys until the baby came. Jim and Dr. Marroquin discussed my condition and decided the baby would probably come about three o'clock.

With the time of arrival of the baby settled, Jim decided he had time to go back for Florence and then he could take all three children back to the house. Traffic was not bad so he then decided he had time to feed the little ones before going back to the hospital. Looking at his watch, he saw he still had an hour and a half, so he laid down by Elizabeth to tell her a story. Then the inevitable happened. He closed his eyes and went sound asleep himself.

My nurse was a little four and a half foot enthusiastic ball of energy who was soon to finish her nurses' training. I asked her where she would be going after graduation. "I don't know yet," she said, "but if God wants me out somewhere in the country I'll go. I am a nurse because I felt that God needed me in that field."

She was taking my blood pressure and temperature as she talked but watching my contractions and the expression on my face with each one. Suddenly, she stopped talking and left the room. In an instant she and the doctor were both back.

It was only one o'clock and all three of us knew the baby was going to beat his daddy to the hospital. I was very upset with Jim at this point and exclaimed, "Where is that husband of mine? I can't wait much longer! Surely he could have gotten back by now!"

"Just be calm, Senora. I don't need your husband to deliver this baby. I delivered both Peggi and Elizabeth, and I've had quite a bit more practice since then. Now, see," he said, "now I've delivered you another little boy."

In a few minutes I was back in my room and Chavela, the nurse, came in with the baby all bathed and wrapped up tight in a blanket. She was talking all the time about how beautiful he was and how wonderful God was to give us another boy. She was sure his father would be very, very proud of him.

"Chavela," I said, "let's play a joke on his father. When he comes in downstairs, don't any of you tell him the baby is already born. Let him come up and find out all by himself. Now go and be sure everyone downstairs knows not to say a word."

When Jim arrived at fifteen after three, he asked at the desk as soon as he entered how his wife was doing. "Oh, just fine," the nurse on duty told him.

Jim entered the room and I pretended to be asleep. "How are you, Honey?" he whispered.

"I'm fine," I replied. "Where have you been?"

"I helped feed the children, then. . . ." A newborn baby's cry came from the bassinet on the other side of the room. "What was that?" he exclaimed as he rushed to look. "Don't tell me it's already here and I missed it!" He started to tell me about going to sleep but then remembered he didn't even know if he had another son or daughter. With that, the nurses came in to chide him for not being there when his son had arrived.

Before I left the hospital with new son Billy, Chavela and I had become good friends. I asked her if she would go to Ometepec to work with us. She promised to consider it seriously.

Two months later, she did join us in Ometepec and became like a member of the family. Her enthusiasm and Christian love impressed everyone and we still consider her one of the finest Christian nurses ever trained.

Madge had decided she wanted to return to Morelia to have her baby because she had some very good friends who would help her when Johnny was not there. There was also an apartment waiting for her near the hospital where their second child had been born. So, soon after Billy arrived, she returned to Morelia. Johnny took a week to help her move. Then, promising to be back before their "daughter's" due date, he rushed back to Mexico City to take a load of materials to Ometepec.

When through the deep waters I call thee to go,
The rivers of sorrow shall not overflow;
For I will be near thee, thy troubles to bless,
And sanctify to thee thy deepest distress.

How Firm a Foundation"— 3rd. verse
Rippon's A Selection of Hymns, 1787

Chapter III

Travel Woes

When Billy was just two weeks old, Jim and Johnny returned to Ometepec with our jeep and trailer and Johnny's four wheel drive pick-up truck loaded to capacity. It took the men three days to reach Ometepec and, much to their surprise, they found many people wanting to work for them. News had traveled fast and everyone knew the two Americans would pay fair wages. They picked two men recommended by the owner of the house as good adobe-brick layers and two as carpenters.

There were no plumbers in the town so Jim and Johnny surprised everyone by working themselves. Men with education and status in life did not get their hands dirty. They should go to Acapulco and hire a plumber!

The men had to make one trip to Acapulco for building supplies, but not to hire a plumber. Don Chico, the older of the two brick masons, had been put in charge of the work and gave them a list of things to buy. He also told them where the best store in Acapulco was and told them to tell the owner that Chico Rodriguez had sent them. With that information the man would sell them good material and not overcharge them for it.

On the way back to Ometepec, they arrived at the town near the last big river. A rough looking man, wearing a pistol in a beautiful holster, approached Johnny and asked in a commanding voice, "Would you give me a ride to Ometepec?" Johnny had been warned against picking up strangers, so he said he couldn't, and drove off. The man walked over to Jim and repeated the request. Fortunately, he remembered the man from the month we spent in Ometepec in 1950. "Why, yes, my General," Jim replied, "If it were necessary to leave the cargo, you would ride

Above: Fording river in dry season—1952. Boys filling water cans.

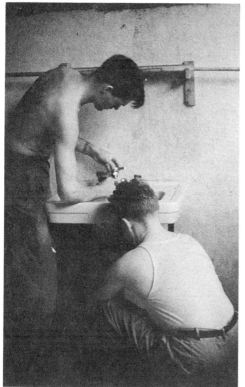

Left: John and Jim working on plumbing.

with me today. I feel honored in giving you a ride."

The General was dressed in civilian clothes but Jim had been impressed when he first met him by his deep commanding voice and his eyes that seemed to look right into your mind. The General chuckled as he climbed in. "Your companion was afraid to give me a ride," he commented. "That's all right. He'll soon know I am in command of this region of the State."

"Oh, yes," Jim said, "I shall tell him tonight and he will be very embarrassed that he did not know you."

Before they reached Ometepec, Jim had learned that the General had run away from home when very young and joined Pancho Villa in Northern Mexico. He had fought for Mexico in the Reformation and was in the raids along the Texas and Mexican border. General Monroe had a son in California who was doing very well and the General liked to visit him. However, he liked his job in Mexico and preferred to stay in Guerrero. He had been sent to Southwest Mexico to catch bandits and cattle thieves. He was known for his toughness with criminals and so far he had made a good record for bringing about order in the region. Jim observed that the General would chuckle once in a while but he seldom smiled and kept a good poker face most of the time.

"By the way," the General said as they approached the edge of town, "some of the people of this town have asked me not to let you come here. I have told them that the Constitution of Mexico stands for freedom of religion. If the devil himself wants to build a church here I will give him permission. Let me know if you have any trouble."

Jim thanked him and the General asked to be let off at the Post Office. The two men shook hands and Jim hurried on through town to unload his cargo. He could hardly wait to tell Johnny about his ride with the General in charge of keeping peace in the region.

"Do you mean the one they call the *Hanging General*?" Johnny asked.

"The very same one," Jim replied. He then told his companion what the General had said about letting the devil himself build a church and the two men laughed. "Just yesterday you were called a devil by the old woman at the corner store," Jim said, "and I was called one by a child in the street, so maybe we ought to get busy and build a church before someone else is sent to relieve the General."

In Mexico City, Madge and I worked on planning food for the rainy season. For about four months, no trucks would be able to travel over the route between Ometepec and Acapulco. The rivers would become deep and wide and the lowlands would be muddy bogs. Airplanes would fly in the morning hours since the rains started usually about mid-afternoon. Air freight was expensive so we had to order as many canned goods and other staples as we could while the trucks were still running.

Jimmy continued to improve and was given extra time in the pool in the afternoon. He was a good swimmer and his right arm began to gain back some of its lost strength. The doctors were pleased with his cheerful attitude and his cooperation with everything they suggested. After three months of therapy he could hold a pencil in his hand and so began the long process of learning to write again.

Florence had suffered partial facial paralysis so, in addition to her therapy at the hospital, she was to chew bubble gum at home and practice blowing bubbles. This she thought was wonderful, but I was faced with a problem. Bubble gum was hard to find in Mexico and I didn't have time to go searching for it.

The pastor of the English-speaking Union Church and his wife came to visit us and I was discussing my difficulties in finding bubble gum. "I'll announce it in church Sunday," he volunteered. "Some of the American families travel quite often to Texas. Let me see what I can do."

The very next week they brought six boxes of bubble gum and both Florence and I were delighted. I had never liked for the children to chew gum, especially bubble gum, and I detested it when the gum came in contact with the hair. However, as I saw the delight Florence had in chewing and blowing, even when her mouth was too crooked to make a bubble, I relented and even chewed some myself to show her how. We saw improvement in a few short weeks and by the time we were ready to go to Ometepec her face was almost normal. Her smile was the first to return and only when she cried could we see the drawing to one side of her facial muscles.

The maid who had worked for the owners of the house we

were using had continued to work for me part-time. She was a fine Christian as well as a good maid. She had a daughter who also worked part-time, so I had somebody helping most all day. Ester, the daughter, had a baby three months old and sometimes she had to bring the baby to work. She was a good baby and seldom cried or demanded attention. She played in Elizabeth's "corral" and watched the activities of the other children.

One day the Grandmother wanted to talk to me. Ester's husband had left them and had gone to Tampico to work in the oil fields. He had told Ester he would send for her, but now two months had passed and they had not even heard from him. Ester wanted a few days off to go see if she could find him. The mother was worried and wanted to know what I thought about it. They had relatives in Tampico and Ester could stay with them. We talked for quite a while. The mother thought Ester's husband had left her for good and did not want to be found. But if I thought it would be safe for Ester to go by herself with just the baby, she would give her permission.

"When I was young no woman would travel by herself. And a baby was not considered a good protection. She should have a man along; her husband or her brother. But Ester says it's different today. She can take a bus early in the morning and be in Tampico by night. I just don't know what to say. She has no brother, and I cannot go. Someone has to stay here to take care of the five children in school."

I told her I thought Ester was a reliable young person, and the bus was not really a dangerous ride as far as meeting bandits was concerned. Finally, after many questions were asked and I had attempted to answer, she agreed to let Ester go. "And, by the way," the mother added, "there is a woman in my church who can come and stay with your children while you go to the hospital in the afternoons. She is a fine lady, honest and good with children. She will come this afternoon to talk to you if you would like to have her."

Lupe came that afternoon and informed me that Ester was packing to leave the next day. She had been almost ready to leave when her mother returned from my house that noon, but was now planning to catch the early morning bus the next day.

At eight o'clock the next morning, Ester's mother had not

arrived, so I began to do the chores, hoping she would come before I finished school with Florence. At eleven o'clock, Lupe appeared at the door and began explaining to me such a tangled story of who did what, that I was completely mystified. After she repeated everything several times, I began to understand a little more about Mexican family relations and the disadvantages a woman has. An uncle from the Gulf Coast had arrived the night before and informed Ester she should not try to go find her husband. The uncle knew where the husband was and yes, he had another woman, and no, he did not want Ester to come to Tampico.

The uncle, being a man, and the older brother of Ester's mother, felt he was the proper one to tell them both what they should do. The uncle also informed them that he was going to look for a job in Mexico City and wanted to stay with them until he found a job. There was much more but I did not understand most of it. Lupe said Ester had sent a little sister over to give Lupe a note asking her to come to work for them today, and the little sister had told all she knew.

That afternoon, just before dark, Ester came hurrying in to see me. "Oh, Senora," she cried, "I don't know what to do. I do not like my uncle, but the family thinks he's right about my not going to look for Jorge. My mother says I must respect my uncle's advice and stay at home. But after you leave I will not have a job and will be under their authority. I will have no money and will be at the mercy of the family. But mother cannot earn enough for two more children. I have been helping her with food even now. I do not want to be obligated to my uncle. As soon as he gets a job, he will send for his wife and five children and I will have to be their maid. He won't pay me because he will say I owe him for his taking care of me." She broke down crying and I tried to understand the ins and outs of a poor Mexican family. All I could give her that night was sympathy, but I would ask around and see if I could find another American family who needed a maid.

The next morning Ester's mother arrived on time and with many apologies. She tried to explain all the family ties and reasons for the way they thought, and I tried very hard to put myself in another culture so I could understand. It is strange, I thought, that we both read the Bible and pray to the same God, yet we interpret things in such a different way. I was not at all prepared for the request this mother made before finishing her well thought out speech.

"Senora, Ester and I both think the best thing for her to do is to go to Ometepec with you. She would be a great help to you as you unpack and start to live in a new town. Her baby is no trouble, as you have said before, and Ester would work hard. She could stay with you until her uncle finds a job here or returns to his own home. In the meantime, Ester can write to Jorge. Maybe he'll change his mind and come back. After all, she is married to him. Please, Senora, take Ester with you for six months. God will repay you for you will be doing a great deed of mercy."

"And what would your brother say about her going with me?" I exclaimed when I could get my breath. She had talked so fast and convincingly I could hardly keep up with her. "Won't he disapprove?"

"We won't even ask him," she declared emphatically. "We will only tell him she is going to help you move and get settled in your new house. I'll tell him the day you leave."

"I will have to write to my husband," I said. "I do not know the condition of everything there. I'll write to him tonight and should have an answer in a week. That will give her a day or two before we leave. "Will that be time enough?"

I wrote to Jim that night but was certain he would think it best to get someone there to work for us. Even so, I didn't dismiss the idea from my mind. Four days later, I was very surprised to receive a telegram from Ometepec saying: "Good idea to bring Ester. Plenty of room. Love, Jim."

Jimmy had been home a week and was to see the doctor two days before going to Ometepec. He had his tenth birthday in the hospital and seemed much more mature to me. He had exercises to do every day and was not to put weight on his right leg, but had become very expert in walking with crutches. All of us were busy cleaning the house, packing the accumulation of books and toys, and talking about our trip to Ometepec. Ester had never flown before and was really in awe of the idea. Jimmy was ready to go long before any of us. Elizabeth pretended she was a plane and ran around the house with her arms outstretched. Ester's mother promised to finish cleaning the house after we were gone.

She would have it ready for the owners to move back into the day after we left.

The alarm sounded that May morning and I rolled out of bed. Finally, we were going to Ometepec. I called the roll: "Jimmy, time to get up. Florence, dress quickly. Peggi, start by yourself and I'll help with your shoes. Elizabeth, let me dress you immediately." Billy slept like an angel while we bustled around getting dressed. "Today we are going to Ometepec," I said enthusiastically, "Daddy will meet us at the plane and we will go to our new house. Isn't that wonderful?"

Ester cooked us a quick breakfast and everyone was in a mood to hurry. I threw the pajamas into the last suitcase and took it to the door with the other bags and boxes waiting to go.

"We're going to be over-weight," I moaned. Eight people, two of them infants, just couldn't get along with less. I would pay whatever it cost and not worry about it.

It was raining when we piled into the car that was to take us to the airport. Not a hard rain, just one that usually means it has set in for the day. I prayed an extra prayer, "Oh, Lord, if that plane can't go today, give me more strength than I have now, for I just won't be able to stand it otherwise."

We were almost late reaching the airport and once there I gave out orders. "Jimmy, be careful with your crutches on this wet pavement. Let us go ahead and you come very slowly. Florence, take Elizabeth's hand. Peggi, take a firm hold on my coat and stick with me. Ester, you follow behind and see if we drop anything."

What a procession we made! I had Billy, a diaper bag and a bag of books and magazines on my arm. Peggi hung tightly to my coat. Each girl had a baby doll and a doll diaper bag just like the one I carried. Jimmy couldn't carry anything in his arms but his beloved camera was slung around his shoulders. Ester, with her baby and two Mexican string bags, followed just behind Jimmy. The ticket agent's eyes became large and round when he saw us and the fourteen pieces of luggage I paid the red-cap to carry.

Bravely, I walked over to the ticket counter and presented my tickets to the gaping agent. He had not taken his eyes off this strange army that had just descended on the airport.

"Will the plane to Ometepec leave on time?" I asked hopefully.

"Ometepec? OMETEPEC?" he asked as if he were not sure he could be hearing correctly. "You are going to OMETEPEC?" he repeated.

"Yes, I plan to go to Ometepec," I smiled brightly to hide my doubts. "That is, if your plane on which I have bought tickets and made reservations is going today."

He took my tickets and told me to sit down until he called me. I looked around hopefully for a seat and just then American Airlines called a flight. As seats were emptied near us, Ester and I found places to sit. Jimmy sat on some of our bags and someone almost tripped over one of his crutches. "Jimmy, pull your crutches up next to you and don't let them stick out where people might trip on them," I called across the room. It was a warning I was to repeat often that morning. Crutches were still new and Jimmy had been confined to a hospital for months. He stared at the people and planes and read all the advertisements in large and small print. And it seemed that those crutches just wanted to trip someone.

We waited and waited and still were not called. At first, the children were willing to sit and watch the people and planes, but after the first hour the little girls wanted to run. I had already taken Billy to the ladies lounge to change diapers, so Elizabeth and Peggi knew where it was. The bathroom song started and it had more verses than "She'll be coming around the mountain."

At eleven o'clock, I thought I would remind the agent we were still there. Of course, he couldn't help but see us every time we paraded past his counter, but just the same, I thought I'd just remind him where we were going.

"The plane to Ometepec," I said bravely, "Do you think it will leave soon?"

Mr. Round-eyes went to talk to Mr. Long-face behind another desk. Mr. Long-face looked at his watch and out of the window at the rain still coming down. Mr. Round-eyes came back with little or no encouragement in his voice. "It will leave at one o'clock. You can go back into town if you want to and call us at twelve-thirty."

Go back into town? With all these children and bags? No,

I'd rather wait, but I had a distinct feeling that he would like very much if we would just get out of sight.

Florence discovered a place they sold candy bars, and immediately said she was starving. It had been a long time since our hurriedly eaten breakfast and I knew they were all hungry. Besides, they were now beginning to fuss. Fussing was worse than running, so I bought them each a chocolate bar.

I should have known better! After all, we had traveled quite a bit, and I had delt with children for ten years now, but I was beginning to feel weak and helpless. I leaned back in my chair and closed my eyes for just a minute. I became wide awake when I heard some tourists say, "This little girl does not like her candy."

There in the middle of the floor was Elizabeth with candy everywhere except in her mouth or stomach. I had forgotten that she did not like chocolate. She had it only once before and I thought she had just not wanted it. She had said, "No like, no like!" Now I knew for sure that she really didn't like chocolate. I picked up as much of the mess as I could and rushed off again to the ladies lounge. I had never realized how much chocolate was in one little bar, or how much fun a child could have smearing it all over herself.

At twelve forty-five, the ticket agent called me over to his desk. "The flight is cancelled," he said matter-of-factly.

"When is the next flight?" I asked, and wondered why I didn't start crying.

"Oh, I mean the flight to Ometepec on this line is cancelled permanently. You'll have to look for another line to take you there. I know of none. Here is your money back."

I turned and looked at my pathetic looking family. They were tired, hungry, dirty but still hopeful of seeing Daddy soon. My head whirled. Then, when I needed it most, the good Lord gave me the extra strength I had asked for that morning. He must have added a good measure of grace also, for I did not collapse. I went back to the children and announced in a forced happy voice, "We are going back to town and spend the night in a nice hotel. We'll get a good dinner and baths and look for another way to go."

Ten year old Jimmy suddenly became the man of the family. Standing up straight, he said, "Don't worry, Mother. We might have scared this airline out of business, but there are others. Look up there at that little advertisement. It's a small company with a long list of little towns it reaches and Ometepec is one of them. I've read it lots of times today. Come on, let's go eat, I'm about to starve."

I called several red caps to help me with bags, baggage and children and my little army marched back out to the street to find a taxi. Thanks to Jimmy's observation, I was able to call the new airline and make reservations for the next day.

The next morning we were once again back at the airport. We knew the airport now and, after settling Ester down with her baby and Billy, with Florence to help her, I once more approached an airline counter. This was a very small company but they had a larger plane and my spirits lightened as the agent immediately checked in my baggage and wrote out the tickets. Their route was different from the former airline and we would have only one stop before Ometepec. The sunshine was beaming outside and my heart was thankful. I didn't even complain when they charged me much too much for my excess baggage.

By nine o'clock we had boarded the plane and were on our way at last.

"Draw Thou my soul, O Christ,
One with Thine Own,
Joyful to follow Thee
Through paths unknown:
In Thee my strength renew;
Give me Thy work to do:
Through me Thy truth be shown
Thy love made known"

Draw Thou My Soul, O Christ, 2nd. verse
Lucy Larcom, 1892

Chapter IV

The Wood Family Arrives

The first stop on our flight was in the mountains of the southwest state of Oaxaca. The small town of Cacahuatepec (Peanut Hill) had worked hard to cut a runway out of the side of a mountain. At first I could see nothing but forest-covered mountain peaks. Then I realized we were descending and I searched the ground for some sign of a place to land. I was sure the left wing was going to hit the cliff, and was relieved when we stopped. Jimmy, sitting on the other side of the plane, turned to me and exclaimed, "Wow, did you see that drop-off? We must be near the top of this mountain range!" We were there less than five minutes as passengers descended and others climbed aboard. We turned around in a space that seemed smaller than two wing-spans, and when I was given a view of what Jimmy had been talking about my heart almost stopped. Then I realized we had a good pilot who had flown this route numbers of times. Soon we were speeding downhill; suddenly the ground left us and we were out over the valley below.

Ometepec was only a twenty minute flight away and I was interested in the number of small villages we could see isolated in the mountains. There were neither roads nor airstrips but many one-lane paths zig-zagging up the sides of the mountains. Donkeys had walked up and down these trails for many years and were the only connection with the coastal plains for most of the villages.

"Ometepec," someone announced and I looked down on the same scene I had remembered from two years earlier. Boys were chasing the animals off the runway and a lone truck sat on the side of the road. A number of people were standing at a distance watching and waiting for the plane to land.

We circled again and I gave my orders: "Jimmy, please be very careful going down those steps. Florence, take Elizabeth's hand and hurry over to those bushes. Duck down, for the dust will be terrible when the plane takes off again. Ester, hold your baby tight and cover her head. Peggi, you hold on to your doll and run for the bushes. Don't stop to look around just run behind those bushes."

The same rusty steps were pushed against the plane and two other passengers debarked first. Senor Reyna greeted me and helped me down the steps. Jimmy held his crutches under one arm and hopped down the steps on his good leg. The children obeyed me and ran for the bushes but the plane turned quickly and the blast took one of the dolls from its owner and rolled it down the field.

I had covered Billy's head but he did not like it at all and began trying to get free. We all stood up, covered with dust and dry cow-dung. "Oh, Mother," Florence cried, "I tried to cover Elizabeth with my doll's blanket but the wind took it away from me. I must find my doll."

Peals of laughter and loud whoops came from the direction the doll had rolled and a group of young boys came bringing the doll. They were teasing one boy because he had thought it was a real baby and had rushed to save it. The truth was that none of them had ever seen a baby doll with eyes that opened and closed. All wanted to see how it worked. About that time we heard the jeep coming and were more than glad to see Daddy come to pick us up.

All the little boys wanted to help put the baggage in the trailer. Jim offered them each a few centavos, and soon we were loaded. I was glad I had not packed anything breakable for nothing was carefully put in the trailer. Some of the boys offered to ride in the trailer and unload it at the house, but Jim turned them down. He insisted no one could ride in the trailer because it was very dangerous. However, we had to stop several times to make them get off.

On the way into town Jim told me apologetically that the house wasn't as far along as he had hoped. The people kept coming to him for medical help and he had been called out several times at night to inject a baby stung by a scorpion. Some of the men were very good workers, but others didn't understand just what they were trying to do.

Johnny had left to help Madge close up in Morelia. They planned to arrive in Ometepec in about a week. Their third child had been another boy, born just five weeks after Billy. Their house wasn't ready either but both houses had a kitchen with a sink installed on two-by-fours and our stoves were connected. "I hope you wont be too disappointed," Jim said. "We have beds up and, at least, we don't have to sleep on cots."

We went about halfway down the main street then turned left down a steep cobblestone street. The children thought that was fun and wanted to know if we were near our new home. "It's not far," Jim said. "We cross a little creek, turn right and we'll be there."

The little creek was only a trickle that time of year, but would be almost a river later on when the rains saturated the dry parched earth.

"See those trees behind this wall," our guide pointed to some tall coconut trees and another I could not identify. "Those are in our back yard. The yard," he said to me,"Is the best thing about the place. It's big, with an adobe wall all around and shady most of the time. I have had a man cleaning it up and I believe it will be safe for the children to play there."

We walked in the front door and I saw what Jim meant by not having everything ready. The walls to divide the largest room into three were only marked on the floor. The back porch had been added, but not screened. The kitchen was a designated area but filled with boxes of utensils and produce we had bought for the rainy season. Some furniture was still in crates, but the dining table was in its place and chairs all around it.

I turned to Ester and said, "Welcome, Ester, I don't know where to start but let's find a safe place for these babies and get started."

Jimmy had already walked through the house and declared that Billy's bed was in the back bed room but was filled with sheets and towels. Our children slept in screened beds up to age five or six, and I had used all of the beds as packing boxes for the move. Everything would have to be taken out carefully to be sure no scorpions had managed to get between the folds.

We unfolded the play pen I had paid excess baggage for that morning, and placed Annita in it. Jimmy and Florence sat on the bed watching Billy while Ester and I began our long day's job. Everything was full of dust, even the cardboard boxes packed with linens I had hoped to use that night had been invaded with dust.

"Let me have enough for tonight," Ester said, "and I will just rinse them out. It is so hot surely they will dry by dark." She pulled a tub under the spigot and while she rinsed I tried to decide where we could hang them to dry. "Don't worry, Senora," Ester called to me. "I see several places. This is the way we wash at home. Go back to the children. I can handle this job."

I had checked out the back yard when I went outside. So I told the older children they could go explore their huge yard if they would stay out of the way of the working men. There were several trees in the yard: coconut, almond, and two other kinds of tropical fruit trees. One was a round yellow fruit about the size of a chinaberry and I was told by many it had an abundant supply of vitamin C. I decided I would get my vitamins some other way, but the children loved to eat those berries. Another was about three inches long, with knots all over it. It was very astringent and puckered up the mouth worse than green persimmons. All the children in the neighborhood loved this fruit and we were glad to give it away. Banana plants and papaya trees grew in the shade of the palm trees. All in all, I was happy about the back yard.

Jim had already built a shed for storing kerosene and gasoline and had several two-hundred-liter drums all ready for the rainy season. Another shed was built for the small electric generator that had been ordered.

The children were happy until someone declared it must be lunch time and all came running in to eat. Jim had arranged with a neighbor to bring lunch every day for him and Johnny, and had told her we would all be needing lunch on the day we arrived. He had astonished her when he told her we would like lunch at 12:30. That was absolutely unheard of in this region. Lunch was not until sometime between 1:30 and 4:00 o'clock, depending upon whether you ate two or three meals a day. He stood firm, though, and at 12:45 she and her sister came carrying in a delicious meal of white rice, black beans and fried bananas. A bowl of tropical fruits was our dessert. Ester had boiled water that morning as soon as we arrived and we made lime juice without ice to drink.

After lunch came that wonderful Mexican siesta time when both humans and animals rest. Donkeys, cows, and dogs find shade to sleep in for a few minutes, and the hammering of nails and chattering in the street is hushed. I put the three youngest in their screened beds, gave Jimmy and Florence books to read, and in a matter of minutes I was sound asleep.

I think I might have slept a week but at four o'clock sharp the men returned to work. The sounds of hammering and sawing and joking brought me back to consciousness and the fact that there was much work to do before dark.

We ate dinner by kerosene lamps and after the little ones were bathed, Jim rocked Billy and sang to him until he was asleep. It took a while for all of us to get bathed and ready for sleep in our clean beds, but we were all tired and agreed it had been a long day. Jimmy wanted to read by lamp light and I warned him about going to sleep and leaving the lamp burning. We had several lessons in blowing out a kerosene lamp. I placed it by his bed and cautioned him to be very careful. This I repeated many times before we finally had our own generator connected and a few electric lights in the house.

During the night, we were awakened by a loud rapping on the window above our bed. "Doctor, Doctor," came a booming voice through the window. "Alacran" (scorpion), shouted the voice on the other side. "Yes, yes," Jim replied, "I'll be there in just a minute. Wait for me."

I could hear several voices outside and saw the flickering light of a pine knot torch. Jim dressed as he mentioned he had told several people he would go out at night to give antivenom shots to those stung by scorpions. The very poisonous stings could kill a child very quickly. They were a night-time insect and would often fall from the ceiling into a bed or hammock. The old woman had called him once before at night and had informed everyone in her neighborhood that she knew how to get the doctor. She would go at night anytime a scorpion stung a child.

The antivenom had to be kept under refrigeration in this

tropical country. We had bought a kerosene refrigerator and shipped it in with our furniture. One shelf had been designated for medicines and Jim had bought a good supply of antivenom for both scorpions and snakes.

He was quick in getting his bag and medicine. Then he slipped out the door to join the small crowd waiting to accompany him to the sick baby.

The next day was a busy one and all of us kept busy. I gave Jimmy and Florence their school books and we decided which part of the back porch was to be their school room. They then arranged the books on their bookshelves and tables.

Late in the afternoon a woman came rushing in holding her hand wrapped in a cloth. "Oh, Doctor," she cried. "I am the owner of that little food stand at the other street corner. I was reaching up for a candy jar and it fell on my hand. It's cut very bad, can you help me?"

We had just unpacked our new plastic-covered sofa-bed, and I told her to sit on that. She hesitated because it was so clean and new, but I assured her we could clean it very easily. Jim carefully unwrapped the hand and turned to me. "I'm going to have to sew it up," he said, "Can you help me boil some instruments?"

It was more of an order than a question, but I thought, "Now that I can do. But he knows I am not a nurse, and look at that cut hand, I cannot do."

"What do you want boiled?" I asked as I started toward the kitchen.

He usually kept some sterilized needles in a stainless steel container ready for emergencies. Now he gave the woman something for pain, then handed me some things to sterilize in my pressure cooker. Then he went back to clean the wound and look for small pieces of glass that might need to be removed.

I finished with things in the kitchen and placed the instruments and needles on a box by the sofa. As I started out of the room, Jim said quietly, "I'm going to need some help with a light. It's too dark and a kerosene lamp won't do near this alcohol. I need that big flashlight I carry in the jeep." I returned with the flashlight and placed it on the floor. "You'll have to hold it for me," Jim said, "Hold it where I'm working."

I picked up the light and with half closed eyes focused it on the cut where he was working. Then quickly I closed my eyes. The light was all right until he finished that stitch. "Put the light where I'm working," he again instructed.

"Jim," I said, "I think I'm going to faint."

"No, you are not. Just forget about your stomach and your fainty feeling and think about this poor woman who needs our help. You are the only person to hold that light and in order for me to sew up this very bad cut, you must hold the light right where I'm working. Don't close your eyes. Just think about what a wonderful job you are doing."

I lived through the sewing up and cleaning up, then told Jim, as I had told him many times before. "You know I am not a nurse. I can help you any other way, but my sympathies are always with the patient. It was all I could do to get through the ordeal this afternoon."

"Why, Honey, you did just fine. It's not bad to sympathize with the patient, and if you would just watch a few more times you could get over your queazy stomach." At this point, I felt like I had my preacher husband back.

The next day we had two letters that gave me great joy. Chavela had finished her training and would arrive on the plane from Oaxaca on Friday. Johnny and Madge were in Mexico City and would arrive on a week from the next Monday.

Our living room was being used more and more by sick people wanting to see the doctor and I was getting quite concerned about the children being exposed to all kinds of diseases. Jim agreed it was not an acceptable situation, and he was looking for a place to rent for his office. The news that Chavela would arrive on Friday made getting an office space more urgent. We asked the leaders of the town if they could give us any information or suggestion, but all shook their heads.

On the Monday the Woods were to arrive, Chavela, Ester and I planned a big dinner to celebrate their arrival. It was our thanksgiving for all of us being together at last. We sang some in English and some in Spanish, and listened to our travel woes. Most of all, we felt a common bond of fellowship in embarking on a new stage of our lives.

Then one day I was looking for material for curtains in a store run by a woman. She asked, "Are you still looking for an office space? I own the house across the street from you that is now being used for storage for my business. If you are interested, I could move things out and you could use the entire house. Of course, I'll give you a fair price on the rent."

When I told Jim of my discovery, he asked Don Chico, the man in charge of our repairs, what he thought about the idea. Don Chico took his time answering, then said rather cautiously, "It will need repairs, but is basically a good house. You should be careful making a deal with Maria. She is a shrewd business woman. Don't let her charge too much."

That afternoon Jim went to see Maria. After two or three hours of bargaining, they agreed that we could use half the house and all the porch, and she could still use three rooms for storage. The house was built around a patio, and the rooms were large, so we were delighted about the deal. Don Chico told us immediately that she had overcharged us. I didn't care as I was so delighted to move the patients' waiting room out of our house. Our prayers were being answered and our hearts sang for joy.

"Christ for the World we sing,
The World to Christ we bring with loving zeal.
The poor and them that mourn, The faint and over-bourn,
Sin-sick and sorrow worn, Whom Christ doth heal. "

Christ for the World We Sing, 1st. Verse
Samuel Wolcott, 1869

Chapter V

Cultural Shocks

That night after we had fallen into bed, I noticed again that the neighborhood was quite loud. One house had a generator and every night played the same country music as loud as their jukebox would play. Another house had guitars and loud singing. It was almost as if they were trying to out play each other. "You know," I started pumping my husband, "there's something wrong with this neighborhood. Do you know what it is?"

"What do you mean?"

"Why all the loud noise at night? Only on holidays do most people have such loud singing and shouting. It sounds like there is a bar in every house."

With that Jim began to laugh. "There is," he said. "Haven't you figured it out yet?"

He lowered his voice to a whisper and said, "We are right in the middle of the red-light section of town."

I was stunned for a second or two, then a shocked voice demanded: "Why didn't you tell me?"

"Well," he began slowly, "Johnny and I discussed it and decided against telling you. These were the only houses anyone would rent us and we just thought you girls would find things out for yourselves. If I had told you, would you have come? Don't you think God can reach us here? Think of all the children in this neighborhood that need our help. Sleep on it tonight and we'll talk tomorrow."

The next day Madge rushed in to see me and pulled me into the bedroom to talk. Seated on the bed she leaned over to whisper. "Do you know what kind of neighborhood we are living in?"

I answered, "Yes, How did you find out?"

"My next door neighbor, that woman who talks in such a loud voice, came to see me yesterday and told me." Madge laughed as she added, "I don't know enough Spanish to understand all she said, but after she talked for five minutes I began to understand. I was too shocked to reply, even if I had known Spanish. I managed to keep a straight face but all I could think of was 'Why didn't Johnny tell me?' That woman told me hers was the most high class house on the block. That only the richest men in town visited there. She herself has three children by three different high society men of the town. I couldn't believe she would tell me all about it, but she did and I didn't know how to answer her."

Madge stopped long enough to catch her breath then said, "What should we do? How can we raise our children in this neighborhood? What will our friends back home think about this? What are we going to tell them?"

"Madge" I said, "I thought about it nearly all night and three things kept coming back to mind. First, we are to try Ometepec for a year and then decide whether we should stay. Second, there are many little children in this part of town who need help. Jim pointed that out to me. Our next door neighbor has four children by the son of one of the rich men. His family won't allow him to marry her because she is below him socially. Her children need medical help right now. The third thing I thought about was that Jesus loves these children and surely He knows our situation. I don't see how we can do anything this year except be sure that our own children stay close to home. I've already decided that for health reasons mine won't play in other people's yards. However, if their children want to play here we will let them. That was our policy when we lived on the upper coast and it worked very well. I'll admit, though, that we were in a much better neighborhood. As for telling our friends at home, you can decide for yourself. I'm not going to say anything for the present. I know some ladies who would write the Board and demand they call us back. Besides, look at the rest of the town and see if you can tell any real difference, except for the loud noise at night. No wonder so many of the women look so sad. You and I are fortunate. Our husbands are faithful and we know it. Our homes are focused on a different kind of life. Let's make our homes happy places to be and I bet some of these people will ask us what we have that they don't. However, I don't think you and I ought to ever again allow our husbands to find houses for us. I bet you and I could have found better places."

"One thing for sure," Madge laughed again at herself,"I know I will learn some words in Spanish I never was allowed to say in English."

"It's not a sin to learn the words." I said, "It's only bad when we use them. How can we ever teach our children this? We'll just have to pray for patience, wisdom and grace several times a day." Madge left and I returned to Florence's school instructions.

More and more patients were coming to our door asking for medicine. Work on our house slowed down to a snail's pace as we sent nearly all the crew to work on the house across the street. Chavela in her cheerful, caring spirit was a tremendous help. She would gather the symptoms of each patient, take blood pressure and temperature and separate those she thought were really serious. Most had malaria and parasites to complicate their reason for coming to the doctor. Malnutrition in small children broke our hearts.

One afternoon, five men on horseback rode up to the clinic screaming for the doctor. One of the men was covered with blood and he was holding a handkerchief saturated with blood over his nose. The men helped their wounded man off the horse and into the office. It was immediately apparent that all five were drunk.

"What happened?" Jim asked as they helped the man onto the examining table.

"We were near Tlaquache," one of the men began. "One of our bulls had escaped and we were looking for him," another man added.

"Let me tell it," the first one said, "I was the nearest to Beto."

"We saw the bull and Beto was going to lasso him when his horse slipped and Beto fell off."

"As he fell, his horse kicked him in the face," they all chimed in together.

"It bled so bad I was sure he would die," one said.

"How much whiskey has he had?" Jim asked.

"Ay, Doctor, who knows?" they all chimed in. "That was all we had to give him for pain and to make him strong for the trip home. It was so bad we all needed strength so we all took a drink," one said. "And every time we had to stop to help him stay on the horse we gave him another drink." Another said, "And we all needed one. Oh, Doctor it was a terrible ride trying to keep him on his horse when he was hurting so bad."

Jim and Chavela told the men they could go home if they wanted to. "I want to keep Beto here for the night so I can watch him," the Doctor told them. "If you want to wait until I have set his nose and sewn up his cuts, you can take a message to his family. All of you don't need to stay."

One of the men remembered that Beto had a cousin who lived in Ometepec. They decided to go tell him and let him be responsible for the wounded man, then they would go on to their village before dark.

Chavela and the doctor began cleaning up the wound and setting the nose. As soon as the doctor gave the local anesthesia and the pain stopped, the whiskey began to take effect and Beto went to sleep.

Beto stayed in the clinic for several days because his cousins who lived in Ometepec thought it would be better for them to take turns sleeping on a cot by his bed than to get him to their house and back every day. Also they wanted to be near the doctor in case anything happened. The patient recovered very well and only had a faint scar over his eye.

Several weeks after Beto returned to his ranch, a nice looking young man appeared at the house looking for Dr. Boyce. Jim invited him in and the young man said, "I am doing my year of social service near the village where one of your patients lives. He was injured while trying to lasso a bull. His horse fell and accidently kicked Beto in the face."

"Oh, yes," Jim replied, "How is he now?"

"He's doing fine but I have heard so much about the case I simply had to come shake your hand. His friends told me about it first, and they declare Beto's face was kicked completely off but that you sewed it back on."

Both doctors laughed and Jim asked, "Were they drunk when they told you?"

"No, but I believe by their tale that they must have been drunk when they arrived here."

Word had indeed been passed around all over the country-side that Beto's face had been kicked off and that Gringo doctor had sewed it back on, and with only a small scar to show for it.

About this time we received word that a pilot of the Missionary Aviation Fellowship would come with Jack McClendon to take Johnny and Jim to survey the villages and the coastal region. We had asked many people about these villages but no one seemed to know the population or conditions in any of them. There were several towns of Black people living in round thatched roof houses. These were descendants of the survivors of wrecked ships taking slaves to Acapulco. Tampico had been the legal entry for slaves but Acapulco was the contraband entrance and no government tax would be charged. The Black people had found the coastal region very similar to their climate in Africa and had settled in small groups. The region at that time was thick with tropical growth and they made their houses just like they had in Africa. Many wild animals roamed in the forests and hunting for food became a way of life. Fishing off the coastal beaches was also a plentiful source of food. Indians of this part of the country lived up higher in the mountains and only went to the ocean once or twice a year, so territorial rights did not concern either class. Both were fearful of the Spaniards and learned skillful ways to avoid them.

Hundreds of years had passed and the Blacks were still living in their round huts and hunting for deer to eat and jaguars whose beautiful skins could be sold for cash. As Mexicans moved into the government of the regions, both Blacks and Indians began to have hard times.

Jim and Johnny were anxious to learn about the villagers' living conditions and their religion. The language of the Blacks was a mixture of their native African language, Aztec and Spanish. We had already discovered that Mexicans from other parts of Mexico had as much difficulty as we did in understanding the people from the coast.

Early on the date they had set, Jim and Johnny were ready to go. Medicines had been packed, thermos jugs filled with drinking water, and Bible story books to give to children were in the jeep. As soon as they heard the purr of a Cessna circling over the city they were on their way to the airport. We were to look for their return in early afternoon before the rains started.

The men returned about four o'clock because the rain clouds were beginning to move in and the pilot and Jack were anxious to return to Acapulco while they could still navigate. They were all excited about the day's survey and had located several landing strips where they could land.

One strip was near a new village of farmers who had moved to the coast from the northwestern part of the state. Their home-land was dry and rocky so the government had promised them land if they would homestead. While Jim and Johnny were talk-ing to the village people who had run to meet the plane, one man came with an urgent request. He had heard that a doctor was in the group of visitors. Would the doctor please come see his son? It wasn't far to his house. Jim and Jack went to see the boy and the other two men stayed to watch the plane. Jack stood just out-side the house while Jim went in to see the sick boy. He was very thin and it didn't take Jim long to know the patient had malaria and typhoid. He had suffered many seizures during the night and the mother said these had happened before. While they were talking, the boy suddenly had another seizure and Jim added epilepsy to the other two diagnoses.

Jim told the parents he could start medicine for the young boy but he would have to see him several times. He would like for the family to take him to Ometepec for several weeks, so he could begin treatment to control the epilepsy. The boy was con-scious and said he wanted to go. Then he looked out the door and saw Jack standing in the doorway.

"Oh, I know that man. He's Senor McClendon from Teloloa-pan. Some of my friends back there go to the church. They gave me the book I read. Tell him to come in."

Jim was relieved to know that the parents as well as the boy could read, so he wrote out detailed instructions for giving the medication he left.

The father returned to the plane with the visitors and promised to take the son to Ometepec as soon as he could arrange for a taxi plane. He was concerned about leaving the boy in town as they were new to the region and did not know anyone in Ome-tepec well enough to leave a sick boy in their hands. Johnny lis-tened a few minutes then said, "Oh, Senor, come to see me when you get there. We have lots of room and maybe we can work something out."

So Panchito joined the Wood family. He recovered quickly from the typhoid and malaria but the seizures, although coming at longer intervals, did not totally stop for months.

More than anything else, Panchito wanted to go to school. He had finished third grade in Teloloapan but the village on the coast had no school. The book he had brought with him was a Bible and he had read it diligently. Johnny was amazed at the Biblical knowledge the boy had acquired by himself.

One day Panchito came to the clinic with two friends his age. He explained to Chavela and the doctor that he had gone to the school and asked if he could enroll. They tested him and said he could, but they were uncertain about his seizures. So he had talked these two boys into learning what to do when he had an attack and he would like to have the doctor's approval of his plan. Jim gave his okay on the condition that Panchito take rest periods in the afternoons. He started in sixth grade at midsemester and finished at the head of his class.

Late one afternoon, Jim was called to the door by a group of men carrying a man in a hammock. They had traveled several hours bringing their wounded companion. Gumesindo had been shot in the knee while hunting down on the coast. They had heard about the doctor who could put pieces back together, so had hurried to bring him. As Chavela worked to clean the man's leg, Jim asked a few questions. "What kind of bullet was used? How far away were the culprits? What had the friends put on the wound? What had they given for pain?" There was no x-ray, so Jim looked to see if the bullet had passed through the leg or was still lodged in it.

Gumesindo (Gume, for short) and his friends were all black and said they were from a village near the ocean. They were feuding with the homesteaders of another village because the land being cleared for farming was taking away their hunting grounds. It was one of the farmers who had shot Gume.

Jim discovered the bullet had passed through the leg and shattered the fibula just below the knee. He and Chavela worked by lamplight after it became too dark to see. The men waited patiently to see what arrangements they could make for their wounded friend.

When the leg was finally in a cast and the doctor could talk to them, it was evident they had a plan. Could the patient stay in the clinic that night if one of the friends stayed with him? The others would return to their village and send Gume's sister to Ometepec to take care of him at night. Chavela and the doctor discussed the arrangements with the men and agreed to their plan. Gume was placed on one of the two folding hospital cots we had and the friend would use the straw mat they had used in the hammock to bring Gume to Ometepec.

The next afternoon the sister arrived by donkey, bringing her own straw mat and extra clothes for Gume. She had no place to leave the donkey so tied him to a large rock in front of the clinic. She had bought hay on the way through town and said that ought to keep him quiet until she could find someone to take him back to the village.

It didn't take Chavela long to realize the sister wasn't very bright. In fact, she could hardly understand anything she was told to do. The food she brought to Gume was sparse and Gume soon told the doctor he was hungry. Chavela came to me and asked if there was anything left from our dinner she might take to the patient. We hurriedly prepared him a tray of beans, rice and tortillas and a pitcher of limeade.

Before twenty-four hours had passed, Chavela and I agreed that the sister was more a bother than a help. As soon as Gume didn't need help through the night we planned to send her home and send food from our kitchen to the patient.

The next morning when Jim was checking on Gume he noticed the sister rolled into a ball in the corner. She was shaking and groaning and seemed not to notice anyone else around.

"What's the matter with your sister?" Jim asked his patient.

"Oh, Doctor, I think she has malaria and is having a chill, but you can't do anything for her. She is a `tono' and cannot take your medicine."

"What is a 'tono'?" Jim asked with interest.

"When she was a baby, the witch doctor took her out to the path to the jungle and left her. The jaguar passed by and their spirits exchanged bodies. A 'tono' is one who lives in a human body but suffers whenever the jaguar suffers. She will have to find the treatment for her spirit with the witch doctor."

"Well, if she has malaria she needs human medicine right now. She looks as if she has fever. Will she let me take her temperature?"

"I don't think so, but she might let the nurse take it." Gume replied.

Chavela was called but as she approached the sick woman on the floor she was quickly told to get away. The woman fought almost like a tiger to keep the nurse away.

"She must go back to the village witch doctor," Gume said. "You won't want her here tonight. Tonight is full moon and she will go to the jungle to find her 'Tono'."

Gume's sister left on her donkey as soon as she was able to walk and we never saw her again. Now we were faced with a patient who became very bored with an inactive life. He could not read, so books would not help. Chavela asked him if he would like to learn to read and his face lit up.

"Do you think I could?" he asked anxiously.

"Of course. Reading is not hard. I will get you a new book just for teaching adults to read and all of us can help you."

Gume proved to be a good student and Panchito and Chavela went by regularly to help him and teach him more. Then one day he wanted to learn numbers and how to add and subtract them.

His leg was getting better, but without an X-ray, Jim couldn't tell how the shattered pieces of bone were healing, so he asked Gume if he could stay until they were sure it was all right to remove the cast. Gume was glad to stay for he was discovering a new world of reading and writing. His brothers had promised to look after things at home for him.

When Gume left Ometepec he took with him several books, notebooks and pencils and said he was going to start the first school in his village. He would not be able to teach much more than reading, writing, and simple arithmetic, but he had learned how to order books and would keep on studying.

In 1946, during the winter vacation between semesters at the University, Jim had been able to take flying lessons in Toccoa, Georgia, and now he was anxious to get a plane. He had noticed the taxi planes going and coming to many villages, and became

Doctor Boyce and "Messenger I," his first plane, arranging with boys to watch plane while he walks into village. Typical landing field on the costal plains.

friends with the pilots. Some of his relatives back in North Carolina and some friends in Texas were interested in supplying the plane. After several weeks of red tape, he finally received permission to take a Piper Cub into Mexico. He now could see the sick, and Johnny could have Bible lessons. This also included teaching children to read and sing.

Singing played a large part in our starting a Sunday School in Ometepec. At first, we gathered our two families together and sang. One Sunday we would meet at our house and the next Sunday at the Wood's house. Soon we noticed the neighborhood children gathered in the street to listen. Then one day we invited them in to join us and switched from singing in English to Spanish. Before we realized it, we had a regular Sunday School and our houses were not large enough to hold the congregation. Finding a house to rent for church service was harder to find than a house for a clinic. All church buildings in Mexico are owned by the government. Owners were afraid the government might confiscate their houses if they were used for religious meetings. Singing in our homes was not considered a religious service, but to have an organized service might jeopardize the house. So while we looked for another place to meet, we sang and explained what the words meant. Many people came who would not have come to a church. They loved music and had never heard four part harmony. Mexican traditional music is three part harmony without the bass.

We were very surprised one day when the daughter of a very influential family asked us to sing a quartet number at her wedding reception party. We asked what she wanted and she replied, "Oh, anything beautiful. People won't notice the words. We just like to hear you sing."

That night the four of us pored over our hymn books looking for something appropriate to sing. We finally found words that could be sung to the tune of Finlandia. It was quite different from the other music at the party, but the people were very impressed and, without our knowing it, another crack in the wall of fanaticism was made.

We've a song to be sung to the Nations
That shall lift their hearts to the Lord;
A song that shall conquer evil
And shatter the spear and sword.

We've a Story to Tell To The Nations, 2nd Ver.
Colin Sterne, 1896

Chapter VI

We Vote for Ometepec

Three months after we arrived in Ometepec, Ester received a letter from her mother telling her she was needed at home. The uncle had decided it was better in Tampico than Mexico City and had moved back. Ester could get a job working part time and help her younger sisters. Ester was also homesick and we felt we should let her return. Getting a new maid would be hard, especially one who could read and write.

Soon afterward while Chavela and I were sitting at the kitchen table one evening working on a list of things needed for house and clinic, we were interrupted by a scurrying at the front door. Then a girl came dashing into the kitchen and threw her arms around Chavela. "Help me, help me," she cried, "they want to kill me. Don't let them catch me. Oh, please hide me," she begged.

I went to the door and saw two men in the street and quickly closed the door.

Chavela calmed the girl and asked her what the trouble was. "My father and that man were drinking and my father owes the man a debt. They were arguing about the debt when my father said he would sell me to the man for the debt. I do not like that man and I said I would not go with him. When I ran out of the house they shouted that they would kill me if I didn't go with him. They are very drunk and I knew they would kill me if I didn't obey. I knew if I could get into your house you would help me. I've heard about how good you are to people who go to your clinic." Tears streamed down her face and Chavela put her arms around her and comforted her. One of the children called me and I went to talk to them, leaving Chavela with the girl.

We made it a rule to offer our visitors something to eat or drink and Chavela saw that this girl needed something to calm her down. Hot chocolate left from our evening meal was on the stove and the girl took it gratefully. Her hand shook as she tried to drink and Chavela watched her carefully. She realized the girl was truly frightened to the breaking point.

When I returned to the kitchen, Chavela motioned that she wanted to talk to me privately. We told the girl to drink her chocolate slowly and we would see what we could do. Jim was in the clinic and we would have to ask him about the case.

"Senora," Chavela said slowly, "that child needs help. She and her little sister with their father and step-mother came into town yesterday and stopped with one of the women up the street. The father began drinking as soon as they arrived and when the other man arrived they drank together. Those men really are dangerous. If you will permit it, I will take her in my room and she can sleep in the bed Ester left. I didn't want to offer it without asking you."

We had given Chavela and Ester the corner room that opened on to both streets, but they had said they would feel safer if we closed both doors and barred them with heavy wooden bars. They would then pass through the children's room and use the front door to go in and out of the house. The room was large and Ester's bed was empty.

"Let me go talk to the Doctor" I said, "Give her some food. If she hasn't eaten since this morning, she must be hungry. I'll be right back."

I explained everything to Jim and he agreed that the girl could spend the night, but we were to promise no more until we looked into the situation more thoroughly.

Chavela and the girl must have talked most of the night for the next day while I was cooking breakfast Chavela whispered, "We need to talk. Can you get away and meet me in the clinic after breakfast?"

I nodded agreement and Florence came in to set the table. This was her designated job and I told her to set another place for we had a visitor.

Our visitor came in just as I said it and I had a good look at her for the first time. She was small for her age, which she had told Chavela was fifteen. Her clothes were worn but fairly clean. She had been to the shower in the back yard before dawn and had scrubbed herself from head to toe. Her eyes were swollen from crying most of the night, but now she was smiling at all of us. "My name is Lupe," she said, "and I am at your orders."

"Oh, no, I can't sit at the table with you," she insisted. "I will wait on you as you eat and I will wash dishes. I can do lots of things."

She would not join us until we started our morning devotions. Peggi passed out the Bibles and when she offered Lupe one, she shook her head. "I cannot read. I have never been to school."

She sat listening to us read and was amazed that even Peggy could read some words. Our guest certainly was not lazy. She washed dishes and scrubbed the kitchen floor while I was starting the children on school work. As Chavela and Jim were starting to the clinic, she stopped Chavela to demand all the dirty clothes. "I can wash clothes very well," she said, "My stepmother and I washed in the river for a living when we were in Oaxaca."

I asked her to watch the smaller children while I went to the clinic. I also instructed Jimmy and Florence to keep an eye on Billy playing in his pen near their desks.

When I arrived at the clinic, Chavela and Jim were already discussing what to do with Lupe. "Oh, she has had a hard life," Chavela said. "Her mother died when her sister was born. They have brothers but don't know where they are. The stepmother is not married to Lupe's father and the two girls are her slaves. Even the little one must beg on the streets. The girls have been beaten many times and Lupe has stayed with them to protect the sister.

"I talked with her most of the night and told her our God can help her if she will let Him. She was very interested in hearing about our God. The woman where they spent the night when they came to town told them we worshiped a strange God who told us to love each other and help each other. She told Lupe that was all right for us, but it would never work in this part of the country."

"What do you think we ought to do ?" I asked.

"You women figure it out," Jim said as he started to see the sick man waiting in the patio.

Chavela looked at me and smiled. "If it's just up to us, and if it's all right with you, I'd like to let her stay with us. I'll take her as my responsibility to see to it she behaves, and you can teach her to be our maid. I'm sure she would work hard for she had me up early asking where she could bathe and where she could start working."

So Lupe became a member of our family and she became a big sister to our children. I soon found out she was also very intelligent.

Late in the afternoon of her first day with us, her father appeared before our house. He would not come to the door, but stood only a few feet away and called for Lupe. She immediately ran to hide. A look of horror had flashed on her face and made me realize how frightened she was.

The children were all in the back yard except Billy. I had picked him up just before I had heard the shouts at the door. Fortunately for me, Chavela had heard the shouts in the clinic and had rushed out to see the man. She quickly stood between him and the door. In her sweet but firm voice she asked him what he wanted. "I want my daughter Lupé." he said menacingly, shaking his fist at Chavela.

Chavela saw that he was drunk and told him to come back the next day when he was sober and they would talk. With that, the man began to curse. He cursed in past, present, and future tenses. He threatened to bring the devil himself to inflict all kinds of evils on us. Chavela quickly entered the house and closed the door. For several minutes he stood there pouring forth his rage at us. Then, when he realized we were not going to open the door, he walked on down the street cursing and swearing at everything and everybody he saw.

Each afternoon he came about the same time. I would send the older children to play in the back yard. As soon as Chavela heard his first shouts for Lupe, she would rush to the house. Lupe would run to their room and hide under her bed until Chavela arrived and told her not to worry. Her father never had nerve enough to enter the house but he didn't want us to forget his hate for everyone inside.

Our year was about over and we began to plan and think about our forthcoming meeting in Morelia and what we would report to the Mission. Both Jim and Johnny felt we should stay in Ometepec. It would be hard to build a hospital in this region but both men thought it should be done. Madge and I both thought we should stay in Ometepec but we were looking forward to better living conditions in a better neighborhood. We prepared our report with much thought and prayer. We also had to think about warmer clothes for all our children as Morelia was much colder than the tropics of Ometepec. Chavela was to have a vacation while we were at the meeting and I asked Lupe if she would like to go to help with the children. Of course she was delighted, but she had no clothes. "Would you like to go up town and choose material to make you some clothes?" I asked without thinking. She looked almost ecstatic with joy, then her face fell and fear came back into her life. "Oh, Senora," she began, "I haven't had a new dress since my mother died. I was given only those worn by other people, but maybe you should pick out the material. I don't know if my father is still in town or not and I am afraid to walk down the street." My heart ached for her and I wondered if she would ever get over the fear of her father. I was therefore very surprised with her action that afternoon when her father arrived to give us our daily dose of verbal abuse. Usually she had run into the bedroom but this time she waited for him to call her name, then she stepped from behind the door.

"Papa," she said in a clear, fearless voice. "I am no longer your daughter. I am a child of Jesus Christ. I have decided to learn about Him and follow Him and you must go away and leave me alone. In this house I am happy and am learning to read. Go away, for I will never go back to your way of living."

The man was drunk but evidently not so much so that he didn't see a change in his daughter. He sputtered and could not think of what to say, so he cursed and went off down the street. The following day a neighbor told us that Lupe's father had packed up his family and returned to Oaxaca.

Our trip to Morelia for the Mission meeting was a pleasant one for all of us. We had been notified by the British-American Hospital in Mexico City that the doctor from Warm Springs, Georgia, would be in the City and wanted to see our children. The date was just two days before the meeting in Morelia, so everything was working out beautifully.

Jimmy and Florence were given very thorough examinations and the doctor was amazed at their improvement. Jimmy's right foot and leg were the most affected. There was no curvature of the spine and he walked with only a slight limp.

"Keep using your crutches most of the time," the doctor cautioned him. "Now and then walk slowly, a few steps at a time, without them."

Morelia was a beautiful old colonial city with some paved streets and many cars. There were other children for ours to play with. Lupe took special care of Elizabeth and Billy so I felt free to attend meetings and listen to the arguments for and against placing the hospital in Ometepec. It seemed that everyone had different ideas and the discussion dragged on for several hours. Then Jim stood up and faced the group.

"Brethren," he started slowly, "We all have our opinions about many places. Now let's seek God's guidance about His place for this hospital. I move we sing My Jesus as Thou Wilt as a prayer and then vote without any more discussion."

This was one of our favorite hymns and we all sang with reverence. When we had finished, the votes were collected, and much to everyone's surprise it was unanimous for Ometepec!

A typical village made like those in the 1700s by ship wrecked slaves on the southern Pacific coast of Mexico.

We were then instructed to return to Ometepec and look for land for a hospital and two homes. An architect from Mexico City was to be contracted and plans immediately drawn up. We were to start gathering materials and contracting for brick.

We were all excited as we returned to the coastal region. The time apart had been good for us and we actually felt all the problems could be solved right away. We had already been looking at property and Jim knew exactly what piece he wanted for the hospital. It was on the edge of town on what was to be the new road out to Acapulco. This road passed the airport and the hospital would be seen by all coming into town. We would have to locate the owner and see if he would sell.

We were met at the clinic by several people waiting to see the doctor. One woman was sitting on our steps and declared she had been waiting the longest. "I came yesterday, and I have said that if you don't see me I am going to die right here on your doorstep."

We all worked late that night. When Jim and Chavela came in for supper the children were already in bed. We felt we had come from a mountain top experience back down to the valley where the sick and the hungry were waiting .

Jim and Johnny decided they had waited long enough to visit the largest Black populated town on the coast, so one morning they packed medicine and books and flew down to see how the people would receive them. The landing strip was on the edge of town, so the two men started toward the main street. People stood in their doors following the strangers with their eyes, but saying nothing. When Jim introduced himself as a doctor he received only grunts in reply. "If there is anyone sick, I will give them medicine," he told several men standing on one corner.

"No one in this town is sick," the men replied.

"Could you tell us where to find your town president?" Johnny asked.

"In his house on the zocalo," was the reply.

At the town President's house, they were told the President was busy and would not be able to see them. Jim made another offer of medicine for anyone sick. Then he and Johnny walked back to the airplane. They were disappointed but agreed they would try again another time.

About three weeks later a man on horseback galloped up to our door just at sundown. "Doctor," he said, "I am from the village down on the coast that you and another man visited last month. The town President sent me to give you a message. He said that if you meant what you said about treating anyone sick, then come to see his wife for she is very ill."

Jim asked a few questions then told the man he would fly down the next morning at daybreak. Jim then spent some time packing his bag with medicines. Jim was almost sure from the man's answers to his questions that the woman had typhoid. There had been a number of patients lately from the coast with that terrible disease. However, he packed his bag with medicines for several diseases.

He left at daybreak, as he had promised, and returned about three o'clock. "Yes, she has typhoid," he reported, "and so does half the village. Some of the people were afraid to take my medicine, but most were very grateful. I promised to go again in the morning to check on them."

The President' s wife and all those who received injections recovered from the typhoid and Jim was invited to visit weekly to see the sick. Johnny joined him and soon a Bible class was welcomed.

Back at home, Jim was told a woman had been waiting for over an hour to see him. Chavela told him that the woman was not sick but wanted to know if he would go down to their ranch on the coastal plains to see a sick maid of hers. She wouldn't tell anyone what the girl had, but wanted to talk to the doctor in private. "She says money is not a problem, and by the looks of the gold she is wearing she evidently has plenty," Chavela added.

Jim left to go see the woman, and Chavela said to me with a twinkle in her eyes, "And I bet it isn't her maid that's sick. She has too much gold around her neck and hanging from her ears. If it were a maid, she would merely send her home. It's not traditional to spend all that money on a maid. I'll wager it's her daughter."

At dinner that night, Jim told us the woman said she had a maid that had been diagnosed as having leprosy. She wanted to know if he would fly down to see her and look at the medicine they had brought from Puebla for her. They had given her a house apart from the other people and really didn't know what else to do for her.

The next morning one of our neighbors came in to talk to me. "Did I see Dona Chito from down on the coast come in to see the doctor yesterday?" she asked suspiciously.

"You tell the doctor that if he goes down there to see her daughter nobody in this town will come to him again. That woman's daughter has leprosy and, according to our customs, the family is supposed to get rid of her. They lived in a nice house up on the main street and have plenty of money. They own a large ranch down on the coastal plains and have lots of cattle."

"Dona Chito knew what the custom was. So the whole family left Ometepec and went down to the ranch. Some time later they came back with a coffin and had an all night watch with mourners and everything. They didn't open the coffin because of the disease. They buried the coffin in the family cemetery lot and even put up a cross. Then the family returned to the ranch.

"Everyone was told it was Maria, her daughter, in the casket but when the family didn't move back to town, people began to wonder. Then one day some cowboys were working in the next ranch and went over to visit.

They came back saying they were sure that Maria was alive. No one told them but they had found out from one cowhand that someone was living in the house over to one side of the big house, and no one was to go near there. The mother carried food over and put it on a table on the porch. Whoever it was living there ate the food. She boiled the dishes before placing them outside so one of the little boys could pick them up. Several other people had been down since then. "We are sure it is Maria in that house. Just tell the Doctor that in this country no one is allowed to live with leprosy and give it to others. If he goes down there, people won't come to see him for fear of the disease."

"Do you mean to tell me," I said when I had a chance to talk, "You people here in Ometepec think they could kill their own daughter if she had leprosy?" I was truly horrified at the thought.

"Oh, yes," my visitor said, "There is no cure for leprosy and so it is the custom to take one life rather then spread the awful disease."

"Well," I said slowly, "I believe there is something now that can keep the disease from spreading. It might not cure but it will keep it from spreading to another person. I'll have to ask the Doctor about it. But I will tell you one thing. If he thinks he can do her some good, he will go down there and give her the medicine. Leprosy is not as contagious as people think."

"We know better. You just tell him he better not go."

I told Jim that night and he just shook his head. "You know," he said, "many times this year I have thought that curing a disease is easy. But how can we ever cure the ignorance and superstition! Of course, I'm going to see Maria. Dona Chito told me to give her a day to get back by horseback. So I am thinking of going tomorrow. You don't need to tell everyone though. Just say I'm in one of the villages on the coastal plains."

The next morning he was ready to go very early and promised he'd be home by early afternoon. Chavela was busy taking care of those she could, and telling others to return in the afternoon. We both wondered what he would find on the ranch. I wondered if he would find the place by the vague directions he had been given. We worried in vain, though, for he returned for our noon meal and was very pleased with his visit.

"They were so grateful for my visit they sent you a cheese that is truly a luxury in that part of the country." It would have to be cooked because it was not pasteurized, but that was no problem. We all liked our "fried cheese" and were delighted with the gift.

"Well, tell us all about it," I said, hurrying him along, "Is she the maid or the daughter? Does she really have leprosy? How bad is it?"

"Chavela was right," Jim said as he nodded her way, "Maria really is the daughter and she really does have leprosy. The medicine she has been given is not the latest treatment, so I will write to the American Mission to Lepers. Dr. Kellesburger will certainly get me the best and latest treatment for her. In the meantime, I'll go down every week to give her the injections that have been perscribed. She is a young girl and very intelligent. She is also very lonely and depressed. I'll get Johnny to go next time. They have many children of workers who are not in school. Dona Chito said we were welcome to have a Bible class. Her son has been to the States as a farm worker for several years. He is back now and is helping them on the ranch. He brought a Bible back from his last year in the States and has given it to Maria. She told me that Job was her favorite book."

Chavela had been listening very attentively and suddenly spoke out, "Oh, that poor girl! She is a prisoner in her own home land. No hope, no hope! No wonder she likes Job." She wiped tears from her eyes as she finished talking and all of us felt as she did.

Johnny did join Jim on the next trip and came back with many ideas of ways to help Maria's situation. He had sung some hymns and songs. Maria was quick and learned them almost immediately. Johnny offered to get her a wind-up record player and some records, to which Maria responded enthusiastically. Maria had stayed in her house while Johnny had a Bible story for the children. However, she insisted that he repeat everything to her while Doctor Jim saw the sick who had gathered under a big shade tree.

The new medicine Jim had written for came in record time. It had been shipped directly from London with full instructions. He was glad to see it was the new medicine and could be taken by mouth. He said, "She is not only intelligent but highly coopera-tive and will keep a record of taking her medicine."

Several weeks after the start of the new medicine Maria was showing improvement. However, her mother said it wasn't only the medicine. "I used to hear her crying in the night and I lay in my bed crying also. Now she sings those songs Johnny taught her and the ones she learned from the records. Now we both sleep with hope knocking on the door."

"Come ye disconsolate, where'er ye languish,
Come to the Mercy seat, fervently kneel;
Here bring your wounded hearts, here tell your anguish;
Earth has no sorrows that heaven cannot heal."

Come Ye Disconsolate, Where'er ye Languish, 1st verse.
Thomas Moore, 1816

Chapter VII

Open Doors

We were all sitting around the table finishing our evening meal one night when Johnny came rushing in. "Jim," he declared, "I must talk with you privately. Finish your supper, then we'll go over to the clinic."

"If anyone is sick I will go right now." Jim offered.

"Oh no, no one is sick. It's just something I have to talk about," Johnny said.

The two men soon left. Chavela and I looked at each other, each wondering if the other knew what was to be discussed. We didn't have time to discuss it then, for it was time for baths for the little ones and games with the older ones.

About an hour later Jim returned with a smile on his face that told me he would talk later about something he considered funny. His eyes twinkled and every now and then he would smile for no apparent reason. I could hardly wait to get him by himself. "Okay, what is it?" I asked.

"You would never guess," Jim said, "Johnny came asking me to teach him some bad words in Spanish. Never did I ever dream I would be teaching a fellow minister curse words."

"Why, for heaven's sake, would he want to know curse words?" I asked.

"Panchito told him that his boys are saying some very bad words and he ought to wash their mouths out with soap. Johnny asked him what the words were and Panchito wouldn't tell him. He said they were so bad he couldn't repeat them. His father had told him to never, never repeat those words.

Then Johnny said to me, `How can I correct my children when I don't even know what it is they are saying? You've been to the University, surely you heard those words.'"

Jim stopped to laugh. "I told him it didn't take a university education to learn to curse but, yes, I did learn a few words." He wrote down some words and said he guessed he would have to teach them to Madge. We agreed it was hard, especially trying to learn correct Spanish in a neighborhood where so much said was what we shouldn't learn. We went to bed laughing, but we knew it really was a serious matter.

About ten o'clock that night we heard voices approaching our house and the very loud commands of our friend with the pine knot torch. "Let me call him," she said, "he knows my voice and will come immediately."

She really didn't need to knock on the window. Jim was already up and dressing. I knew I wouldn't get back to sleep until he returned so I slipped on a house coat and shoes and went to my desk to write some letters.

Suddenly the air was alive with awful noises: screaming, drums, buckets and pans being beaten. Donkeys began to bray and dogs barked and howled at the unusual noises. I ran to the front door and was joined by Chavela, Jimmy and Florence. My first fear was that Jim had been ambushed. I saw the neighbors running past the house and one of them stopped to tell us what was happening.

"It's the `clees', she yelled above the noise. "Look up at the moon. The `clees'. If he eats the moon the world will come to an end. Come on, we must be in the church if the world ends."

"It's just an eclipse," Jimmy answered. "It will be over in a few minutes."

"Why all the noise?" Chavela asked.

"Oh, everyone must help scare the 'clees' away. Especially the pregnant women. If they don't bang pans and beat buckets their babies will be born with a harelip. I've got to run. The moon is more than half eaten now, and I want to be in the church just in case anything happens."

We stood in the door watching the neighbors run toward town and I wondered where Jim was. He returned about a half-hour later and was not at all surprised to find us sitting up waiting for him. "I'll bet you weren't as frightened as I was," he said. "We were on the worst street in town when suddenly people ran

out of their houses beating buckets. The old woman told me not
to be afraid, that it was only a `clees' and she had lived through
many of them. Only young women should worry because if they
don't make noise their babies will be born with a harelip."

" Where do you suppose they ever got those weird ideas?"
he asked Chavela.

Lupe spoke up, "It has something to do with their Sun and
Moon Gods, but we were never told why it would happen; just be
sure to make noise. The bucket is from the Indian custom of
sending messages and has a special rhythm. It can be heard very
far away and tells everyone else to start beating pots and pans."

Jimmy had looked up his book on the sun, moon, and stars
and showed us the list of dates and eclipses. He showed the picture to Chavela and Lupe. Chavela said he should show it to our
neighbor the next morning.

Early next morning as we had expected, our neighbor
appeared at our door. "How did you know the moon would
return last night?" she asked in a puzzled tone. Jimmy had his
book ready and soon several children had gathered around to
look at the pictures and ask questions. Jimmy and his book were
very popular that morning and I was glad to let him explain
nature while I took care of my routine jobs.

Madge and I decided we would take afternoon walks and
look for a possible site for the hospital and homes. Word had
been spread abroad that we were planning to build a hospital.
We heard also that a certain group of very fanatical religious people in town had planned to stop the city council from allowing us
to buy land or build.

We were not really concerned as we knew that if God wanted
us to stay He would overcome all other obstacles. However, we
were surprised and rather chagrined when we heard that a group
of the madams from our neighborhood had been to the city leaders to speak in our behalf. One of our neighbors told us that they
had heard about the opposition to our building a hospital. They
decided to go in a group to tell the City Council not to listen to
those people. "We told them that when those fanatics and the
City Council all lived as good lives as you do, then they should be
heard. But you people have come in here and helped us in sick-
ness and been kind to our children. We told them off. Si,

Senores, we told them they should help you instead of criticizing."

We thanked them for their concern and their good words for us. Then I felt a little guilty for not wanting to live in their neighborhood. "Lord," I prayed, "let me be more humble. Help me to love these people but hate the kind of lives they lead. Help me to look at them through your eyes and above all, Oh, Loving Father, help me to train up my children to understand right from wrong without hating the wrongdoer. It's wisdom we need, Your wisdom."

"Ola, Doctor," a voice called from the front door. "May I come in? I have something I think you will be interested in."

We invited him in and he introduced himself as Ramon Reguera, a dentist in town. He had a package wrapped in old newspaper under his arm and when he reached the dining room table he began to unwrap it. "This book belonged to Captain Cary Brenton of the Royal British Navy. He died here in Ometepec and my Aunt Rachel took care of him in his last days." He handed me the Bible. On the first page was written in beautiful old handwriting, "Captain R. Carey Brenton, British Royal Navy, Brigadier of the National Mexican Armada." On the back of the hard cover was written in large letters, "The entrance of Thy Word Giveth Light. "Ps. 119:130 "

"How did he happen to die here?" I asked.

"He had resigned from the Navy and had come here selling Bibles. He was sick when he reached Ometepec and was unable to continue his travels. He had been lent to President Porfirio Diaz by Queen Victoria to start the Mexican Frigate School. He served in this capacity for five years, then decided to become a missionary to southwest Mexico."

Jim was looking over my shoulder and exclaimed, "Look how he studied his Bible. And look, those are prayers in the margin. Honey, this is the Bible that Mr. Webb, the English missionary in Mexico City, told us about. He said he thought it was still in Ometepec."

We both became excited as we read Psalm 2:8, "Ask of me and I will give thee the heathen for thine inheritance," and beside it, penned in the Captain's beautiful handwriting, was the prayer "Lord Jesus I ask of thee for West Mexico converted to Thee as my heritage." Page after page was marked, and a personal comment or prayer was written in indelible pencil in the margin. Jim and I were so fascinated with the Book we almost forgot our visitor.

"Senor Reguera, we will give you another Bible if you will let us keep this one for awhile," Jim said when he realized that he was almost being rude to our guest.

"Do you mean to say I am educated enough to read the Holy Book?" Senor Reguera asked.

"If you can read at all, you are educated enough to read this Book," Jim said, "And if you pray for guidance to understand what is written, God will give you His blessing and understanding."

Our visitor shook his head slowly, then said, "I have kept this book for thirty years without reading it because I was told I would have to go to Seminary to be educated enough to read it. Yes, you may keep it awhile, and I would be very grateful for a new one to read. Captain Brenton was a very fine man, and my Aunt Rachel knew he was a believer in a God of love."

I went to our box of Bibles we had to sell and found a leather bound, nice size print to give our new friend. He thanked us and left with his new Book tucked under his arm.

A few days later, a young boy delivered a telegram to us and stood waiting while I read it. (It was their custom to wait for you to read a telegram to see if you wanted to send a reply.) As I was reading, Florence was practicing the piano and the young boy was fascinated. He slowly backed up to the piano and touched a key. Florence had stopped playing when she saw him reaching out to the keys, so when he struck a note it sounded loud to him. He jumped and looked very guilty but Florence and I just laughed. "Do you like music?" I asked.

"Oh, yes," he replied, "And I hear that you sing on Sunday afternoon here or at the other house. Can anyone come to your classes?"

"Of course," I replied, "We would like very much to invite anyone who loves music to come sing with us."

"I live with Senor Reguera, just across the street from the telegraph office," he said. "I will come Sunday, if I can." The boy, Ignacio by name, but affectionately called Nacho by everyone, did indeed join our growing Sunday School. He was quite musical and learned the hymns quickly. Soon he was going with Johnny when he did not have to work. At night, he would read the Bible to Senor Reguera and his wife. Before long, they also, joined our Sunday School.

One afternoon as Madge and I were walking on the edge of town, she stopped and exclaimed: "See that beautiful big tree? Wouldn't a house in the shade of that tree be wonderful? Just think of the view!"

"The view would be marvelous. But, Madge, how would you ever get water up to your house?"

"Pumps," she said without hesitating, "One at the foot of the hill pumping to a water deposit and another pump there to pump the water to a deposit on the top of the house. I'm going to tell Johnny to start to find the owner of the land."

We were still trying to find the owner of the lot Jim wanted on the main road, but he didn't have much time to ask anyone except God for information. This he did often, but the sick were coming in greater and greater numbers and at times I wondered if we would ever move out of our large but inadequate house.

One patient, a woman with malaria and typhoid had come several times for treatment. A week or two after she was well she returned to ask Chavela if she could talk to the Doctor. "I'm not sick,"she said, "I just have something I want to discuss with him. I can wait until my turn to see him."

"Doctor," she began when she was finally ushered in to see him, "I have a piece of property on the edge of town and I would be willing to sell it to you if you want it. I know you have been looking for land to build a hospital. I also know that I will have a great deal of opposition if some of my friends find out I am offering my land to you. However, I know we need a hospital and I know you will be honest with us. If you want to see the land I would like for you to do it without saying anything to anybody about my selling it. You have treated me and several members of my family, and I feel like I should sell you this land if it is suitable. If we can get the preliminary steps taken before anyone finds out about it, I can handle the criticism I will have."

Jim told her he could not say anything until he saw the land, but he would certainly like to see it. She began to tell him just where the property was.

Jim could hardly believe his ears! The more she talked, the more he realized it was the very piece of land he had been wanting but couldn't find the owner. Here the owner was, a patient he had been treating for several weeks, and she was almost putting the land in his hands.

He came for the evening meal and had a look of joyous unbelief. He called me aside to tell me about it and shaking his head he exclaimed, "Look what God has done!"

A neighbor's house next to the lot bought for hospital. Typical house of the rural community.

We had a hard time not telling anyone about the incident. The next day we drove past the banana plantation and looked at the markers she had told us would be there. It was indeed the choice piece of land that Jim had wanted, and it was larger than we had ever hoped to find. We were truly awed by the way things had been worked out by a greater hand, more powerful than ours.

It took several weeks to find a surveyor to measure off true boundaries. Then there was the official buying by the representative of the holding company in Mexico City. When the news broke that Maria had sold the land to the foreigner, she was verbally lashed by a number of her friends. She withstood the opposition by holding her head up and saying: "We need a hospital and he is a good doctor. We should be glad he is willing to stay here."

We asked the Woods to come join us for a private thanksgiving service the night we heard that the deal had been finalized and they came bringing more good news. They had found the owner of the lot Madge had wanted and were to talk with him the next day. His being willing to talk to them about the land was encouraging. Furthermore, the house was only about two blocks from our house.

By this time almost two years had passed since we had taken up residence in Ometepec. Now we were ready to start collecting material to build. Brick was made by hand all around the town but it took time. A large kiln would hold only 1000 bricks and some of them would break in the firing. Donkeys would haul them into town, but that also was very slow. Each donkey would carry two baskets with nine bricks in each basket. Usually a man would have only eight or ten donkeys in a train. It would be very hard for the local kilns to produce the number of bricks we needed, and even harder for them to be hauled into town. "Lord," we prayed, "We need another miracle." We were going to see many miracles before we finished these projects.

On one of Jim's trips to the coastal plains, he was impressed with the size of the trees the homesteaders were cutting down and burning in order to clear fields for crops of corn and beans.

"Why are you burning those beautiful trees?" he asked one of the men.

"What else can we do with them?" the man asked. "They are too large to saw by hand and there are no sawmills within miles. Certainly we can't haul them out by donkeys. What do you suggest?"

"We could use them in building the hospital, but I agree with you, it would be impossible to haul them out with what we have. But please don't burn them right now. Let me see what we can figure out."

"They are yours, Doctor, if you want them. We don't have to burn for several weeks yet."

That night Jim and Johnny talked at length about various ways to get logs to Ometepec and saw them into lumber after they were delivered. They decided that Jim should write to an authority on sawmills in Corinth, Mississippi.

Mr. Jones was an elder in the First Presbyterian Church of Corinth, another church helping start this new station. I also wrote to all six of our supporting churches and asked for prayers for our building plans.

On our last trip to Dallas we had met Dorothy and DerWayne Scoggins. He was an officer in the Oak Cliff Church and she was active in the Women of the Church. They had five children about the same ages as ours, so the two families became lasting friends. Dorothy was a good correspondent and kept me up on exciting events in the church there. Soon after Dr. Currie, Pastor of the Oak Cliff Presbyterian Church, had received our letter, he also had one from Mr. Jones in Corinth. He then went to see the Scoggins, who built pressure tanks for gases and chemicals. Dorothy's letter to us continued:

"His news was that a gift of a portable saw mill had been made for the hospital by Mr. Jones. Dr. Currie thought that since we sent loads of LP gas tanks to dealers in northern Mexico we might be able to arrange transportation at least part of the way for the saw mill. We talked it over, and Wayne and I said we wanted to be doers of the Word and not hearers only. Dr. Currie led us in prayer for the solution we needed.

"In the following days, we talked with our friends, customers, and suppliers about our new project, and surprising things began to happen. One of our buyers from Alabama told me he had an old International truck he would give us. It was in use but he had been considering trading it in. The next week he sent the truck over, and our company mechanics restored it to its best possible condition.

"The truck would not only provide transportation for the sawmill, but once there, by the use of a power take-off, its engine could provide the power to run the saw. A salesman from one of our suppliers made us a gift of a heavy-duty winch which could lift heavy timbers onto the truck bed. It was installed onto the truck. Our painters gave it a coat of bright red paint, and the old truck looks good!"

Soon after Dorothy's letter arrived Jim was on his way to drive the truck with its precious load to Ometepec. He was in a hurry to get back before the rains started. He borrowed a truck

Truck "Dorthea" loaded with sawmill. Dignitaries at dedication: (left to right) Julio Diaz, Company rep. in Mexico; Dr. T.W. Currie, Pastor of Oak Cliff Presbyterian Church; Dr. William Elliot, Pastor of Highland Park Presbyterian Church and Chairman of Board of World Missions, (Presbyterian Church U.S.); Mr. and Mrs. DerWayne Scoggins; The Hon. Ernesto Zorrilla, Consul for Mexico in Dallas.

similar to the one he would be driving and practiced driving it in their parking lot. He had told everyone that in Mexico all trucks are given names, usually a feminine name, and this truck was now named "Dorotea" (Dorothy) for Mrs. Scoggins. A slogan was usually painted on the front bumper, so the painters put on the final touches with "Dorotea" over the windshield and "Dios Bendiga Ometepec," (God Bless Ometepec) on the front bumper. Before the paint was dry, Jim was on his way.

It didn't take him long to discover that the gear shifts were not exactly like those on the truck on which he had practiced. He practiced long enough to drive out of town, then practiced shifting until he felt fairly secure to continue.

He was worried about two problems: driving through Brownsville and securing a permit to take the load into Mexico.

He solved the first by driving through Brownsville in low

gear, and found the second had been solved for him by some unknown friend. Dorothy told us later it was a Catholic priest in Dallas who had heard about the sawmill and wanted to be sure there was no problem on either side of the border. He had "connections" and used them in our behalf!

All problems were not over, however, for in 1955 the rains started early and with great force. Hurricanes hit the Gulf coast, taking out sections of the highway to Mexico City, and tropical storms drenched the Pacific side of Mexico. After some long, hard detours, Jim finally reached Cuernavaca. Here he talked with a friend who had a printing business. After hearing from the traffic department that it was impossible to reach Ometepec by land, the friend invited Jim to leave the truck in his garage until after the rainy season.

Jim flew in from Mexico City the next day and declared himself an expert truck driver. He was disappointed, of course, that he could not deliver the truck all the way home, but was thankful that the way across the border had been opened and the truck was more than half way to Ometepec.

Holy Spirit, Power Divine,
Fill and nerve this will of mine;
By you may I strongly live,
Bravely bear,and nobly strive.

Holy Spirit, Truth Divine
Samuel Longfellow, 1864

Chapter VIII

Two Steps Forward, One Step Back

Soon after Jim returned from his trip for the truck he was awakened one morning with loud knocks on the door and shouts of "Doctor, come, we have a wounded man."

In the street were several men, two of whom were carrying a hammock tied to a long pole. They had traveled several hours, stopping now and then to change the load to two other men.

The wounded man was unconscious and Chavela and Jim hurried to open the clinic and examine the patient. One of the men stopped to tell me how the man was hurt. He was in a terrible fight. He and some"friends" had started drinking early the night before and about ten o'clock at night had started arguing. Then this man and another one started fighting with machetes.

"He is badly hurt," the man added. "Both hands are almost cut off. He has bled quite a bit, too."

"Where were you?" I asked. "Why did it take you so long to bring him to a doctor?"

"Oh, we were over in Oaxaca and at first we thought he was going to bleed to death. Then someone told us we should bring him to you because this Doctor can sew people back together."

The man left to join his friends and I went to prepare breakfast for the family. Several hours later, Chavela came in and motioned to me that she wanted to tell me something. I left the children and we went into the bedroom. She was worried and anxious about something but I was not prepared for what she had to tell. "The wounded man is Lupe's father," she said, "he is in very bad condition and I want you to go with me to tell Lupe. The doctor worked hard to sew everything back, and now he has casts on both hands."

Local "ambulance" arrives at our front door.

Telling Lupe was hard, but she took it better than I had expected. "Is he going to die?" was her first question and "Where is my little sister?" the second one. One of the men told us that the little sister and the wounded man's woman would be getting into town today. Our big question was: Who will take care of this true reprobate of a man?

Lupe looked down at her father as he began to regain consciousness. This was the man who had beaten her as a child, tried to sell her for his alcoholic debts and threatened to kill her. She didn't tell us her thoughts, but she took the water from Chavela and offered to spoon it into his mouth.

The next two days were hard for all of us. Lupe took food to her father and was cursed for everything she did. When he realized she was truly feeding him good food, he asked for a drink of liquor. His woman came by the clinic to see for sure that he was still alive, then left. The little sister came to see Lupe, but had been told not to enter our house. She was a pathetic sight! Hair uncombed, ragged clothes that didn't fit, and a sad, almost hopeless look on her face. Lupe asked my permission to feed the child. I told her not only to feed her, but bathe her and put on clean clothes. As she was not allowed to come into our house, Lupe took her to the back patio of the clinic. We looked for some clothes from our three girls, and after awhile a clean, different-looking child came out. I could not help but notice, however, that her eyes were still sad. She did not smile.

The stepmother came that afternoon to take the child with her, and we did not see them again for two days. The woman told Lupe they were taking a room up the street and the sister could come to our house to eat in the afternoon. The step mother had a job washing clothes, but there would be no food for the girl.

So every afternoon for about two weeks, Chica came to see her sister. Lupe bathed her, combed her hair and taught her to say John 3:16. "If you ever want help, find someone who knows this verse and ask for help," she instructed her sister over and over.

As soon as the stitches were out, the wounded man took his woman and child and went back to the state of Oaxaca. We never saw him again.

For us 1954 and 1955 were very busy years. The Woods were able to buy the land they wanted and had started their house. They had decided to build of adobe brick as it was more available and faster to build. They were to leave in the spring of 1955 for a long overdue furlough. A young building engineer from Texas was coming to help with the building of the hospital and house. The architect from Mexico City brought a "maestro" builder and some good bricklayers with him.

Johnny and Jim loading the jeep.

Jim and Johnny had done a good job of plumbing on our houses in town but had no desire whatsoever to extend their knowledge or craftsmanship in this line. Jim finally found a plumber in Acapulco who said he would take the contract, but his young nephew would do the work. The uncle would be responsible, make periodic visits to check on the work, and make major decisions. His nephew, Tito, was well trained but still young. He lacked the experience of overseeing a large job, but the uncle had total confidence in his ability.

Tito was young, with broad shoulders, and a wide smile. He looked as if he could enter any boxing ring and come out winning. It did not take us long to find out that he was a very devout Christian and enjoyed his Christian life. Before the hospital was finished Tito returned to Acapulco and married a young girl as happy in her Christian life as he was.

Also before the hospital was finished, the town officials asked Tito to make Ometepec his home and become the town plumber. Bella, Tito's wife, became one of the leaders in the women's work of the church, and Tito was one of the first elders.

The Federal Government was trying to start the highway into Ometepec and had an old bulldozer and small crew coming through the jungle marking off the road. When the workers all had malaria, they sent for Jim to please go help them. He flew down and took medicine several times. They wanted to do something for him in appreciation, so when they saw our workmen trying to level the hill top by hand, they offered to bulldoze it with the giant machine. In one weekend they gave us at least a month's headstart on the project.

As soon as they thought they could ford the rivers, Jack, our friend from Teloloapan and Gayle, the young engineer from Texas, picked up "Dorotea" in Cuernavaca and started for Ometepec. When they reached the river at Marquelia, about fifty miles from Ometepec, they got stuck in the sand. Then, in trying to back out, the axle broke. Jack stayed with the truck while Gayle borrowed a horse and rode to the nearest telegraph office to send a message to Jim for help.

Jim flew down to look for them, landed on a straight stretch of the new road, flew the axle to Acapulco to be sure he would get the right size, then returned to the broken down truck before sundown. "Dorotea" received a royal welcome when she finally reached Ometepec.

Very soon thereafter, the men went for a load of timber down on the coastal plains. The local people could not believe how easy it was to load the truck with the help of the winch.

In Ometepec, when the men set up the sawmill, people came from miles around to watch. They had used a hand pulled pit saw for generations and this looked like a miracle to them.

When Jim was called from the clinic to look at some problem at the building site, patients would grumble, but usually   come back later. We tried to close the clinic, but that,too, was unsatisfactory. Jim worked from sun-up into the night and often he and Chavela were called at night to sew up some machete wound, or see a critically ill person brought in from some surrounding village.

When Gayle arrived, and the sawmill was working, things went faster, except for those days when the rains started early. Long, heavy beams for holding the roof had been ordered from some men up in the mountains where they had tropical mahogany trees. They had promised to deliver them in March, but now in April they still had not been delivered and we could not even get in touch with the men. Not all the brick had been delivered either, and frustration over delays made several bricklayers from Mexico City want to go home.

Then one Sunday morning we were awakened at sunrise by loud shouts of men driving animals. We heard hard knocks on our door and calls of "Doctor, your beams are here."

I opened the door and could hardly believe my eyes: teams of oxen, each pulling two wooden beams, filled the street as far as we could see. "Where do you want us to put them?" the leader asked.

It was a little over a mile to the building site, so Jim said he would go with the men to show them where to unload. What a sight they made trying to turn those oxen around. Such shouting and laughing had not been heard on our street since we had been there.

It was past Sunday School time before Jim returned, but we all gave thanks that the roof would soon be on the hospital and house. The "maestro" and Gayle went to check out the beams and pay the leader of the crew. Gayle returned saying they were the most interesting beams he had ever seen. He was sure they would hold up the heaviest of roofs. The beams had been sawed by hand, but how they did it we could never understand.

Then came the biggest disappointment of all. Money to finish the hospital would be delayed for several months. All our plans were thrown into turmoil. If we could not pay the men from Mexico City, we would have to let them go. The architect came down and we discussed the problem with him.

After long hours of talking over all angles of the situation, they decided to finish the surgical wing of the hospital, the office, and one or two patient rooms. The rains would soon be starting but they would have the roofs of hospital and house finished.

We would move into the new house before it was finished, and Jim would start seeing patients in the new offices as soon as he could move in.

Then someone suggested that we take our furlough in 1956-57 instead of waiting until 1957-58 when it was due. The Woods would be back in June and we could leave in July. This would eliminate the necessity of starting in the new place, then having to leave in just a few months. Also, the architect said he would make periodic visits to check on the small local crew we could keep working.

Another family problem was facing us also. Jimmy was finishing eighth grade, and we felt he should return to the States for high school. We had written to many boarding high schools, and found them either beyond our financial means, or not well equipped in sciences. Jimmy wanted to study physics. In fact, that was about all he talked about. He read every magazine or book about science he could find when we went to Mexico City. One military school offered him a scholarship but, because of his polio, we had to turn it down.

Then one day we had a letter from relatives of Jim who were not only educators but very good friends. Louise asked if we would leave Jimmy and Florence with them after our furlough. I couldn't believe she really meant it. Nevertheless, I answered her letter in great appreciation and suggested we think it over until we could talk in detail.

The young people of the church were growing and planning

ahead also. Panchito was finishing secondary school in 1956. He had made the highest grades in his class every year and was a leader in the church activities. Nacho was following close behind him in school and was first in his class academically and socially.

In the summer of 1955, a group of young people from the United States were to have a summer work camp at Teloloapan and wanted some Mexican young people to attend also. Because the Mexico City school system at that time did not have vacations in the summer, we were asked if anyone from Ometepec would be able to go. Panchito wanted very much to go so he could learn more English, and plans were made so he could attend.

The young people from the U.S. were very impressed with Panchito. They worked together, played together, sang together, and learned about each other's dreams and future plans. By the time they left, Panchito had been encouraged to apply for an International Rotary Club scholarship to study in the U.S.

You can imagine my concern when I received a long questionnaire to fill out regarding a scholarship for Panchito to attend Jacksonville State University in Alabama. How could he go when he had finished only ninth grade in Mexico? I was also concerned about his epilepsy. He had not had a seizure in several months, but I felt I should tell them about it. In every other way I knew he would do fine. Jim and I both recommended him highly for the scholarship, and several months later he received notice he had been accepted. We then began to inquire about summer school in Texas for him so he could become more fluent in English.

Lupe announced she wanted to be a nurse and wondered how she could go to school. At fifteen, she wanted to start in first grade, if that were necessary to go to nursing school later. Chavela and I both had been teaching her basic arithmetic, Spanish and reading. So we decided to send her for placement testing. We celebrated when told she could enter fifth grade!

Then Jim and I decided it would be better for her if she would attend school in Cuernavaca where there was a Mission home for students attending government schools. This would give her more time to study and she would not have to work as many hours as she was working with us. We did not want to give her up, for she was truly a member of the family by now. Nevertheless, to see the joy in her face as she made clothes and packed to go to school made us rejoice with her for the opportunity.

Chavela was applying to work at the British-American Hospital when we went to the States. The clinic would be closed for a year.

People began to hear that we were leaving for a year and many declared we would not return. Patients poured in from villages all around Ometepec. Some walked in, some rode donkeys, some flew in on the DC 3's or the small taxi planes. All begged us not to leave. It was very hard for Chavela and Jim to attend to all who came. I felt almost guilty for looking forward to a change of pace. Jim was working so hard he hardly had time to spend with the family. We usually started the day together at breakfast, followed by our devotional. All too often,however, we were interrupted by some emergency.

One piece of equipment Jim wanted very much was an x-ray machine. We had finally been able to get one into Ometepec and then had to wait several weeks for the technician to come to install it. The day before it was to arrive, Jim was called to see an Indian with a broken arm. The poor man knew only a few words of Spanish and he knelt before Jim and pleadingly said, "Please, Doctor, it hurts."

Jim immediately saw it was a gun shot wound and asked the man what happened. The man answered in Amusgo, then repeated, "Please, Doctor, it hurts."

While Jim and Chavela were working on the man, some soldiers came by carrying a body rolled in a straw mat. They went on up the street toward the cemetery. Following the soldiers was a group of Indian men. Two of them stopped at the clinic. One man knew Spanish and explained that the wounded man and his son were coming into town with two five gallon buckets of lard to sell that morning and were ambushed. The man's son tried to defend the lard and was shot. The father jumped to protect the son and he too, was shot. The bandits took the two buckets of lard and fled. The young man had died. The friends who were following them told the father to come into town to see the doctor. They would call the soldiers to look for the bandits.

After the wounded man had been treated and put into a cot on the porch, his friends gathered around his bed and talked in Amusgo. The father cried bitterly. When Jim tried to keep him from getting out of bed, he grabbed the Doctor's hand and said in Spanish, "My son, killed, my son, killed."

The interpreter for the group explained that the man wanted to go to see about burying his son, but the others thought it would be dangerous for the man to go outside now. He had seen the bandits and they might try to kill him. Jim explained to the friends that the man should not leave yet as he had been given some medication that would make him sleepy and he might fall and hurt his arm again.

There was definitely a language problem, but they seemed to have the same idea: the patient should stay in the clinic and they would take care of the burial of the son.

The next plane into Ometepec brought the technician to install the x-ray apparatus. The wounded Indian was the first patient to have an x-ray taken in Ometepec. We often wondered what the poor man thought as he was being put under that big black machine, but he never once objected nor complained.

When his friends came by that afternoon, they once again gathered around the bed to talk in Amusgo. They evidently explained the funeral of his son and showed him some official documents. The poor father cried again and the men talked some more.

Then the visitors were quiet while the patient told them about the x-ray. The interpreter went to Chavela and asked what the treatment was they had done that morning. The patient had told them he had been put under a big black machine, and the doctor had shown him a picture of his broken bone. The men wanted to know if they could see the picture, for they could not believe what the man had told them.

Jim took the x-ray and held it up for the men to see, then explained to the interpreter so he could repeat it in Amusgo. They exclaimed in amazement many times and asked the doctor to tell it again. They went in to see the x-ray machine and slowly walked around and around it.

Then the men asked the interpreter to speak to the doctor for them. "No wonder people say the doctor is good," one man said,"when a bone is broken he can see below the skin. We never believed it, but now we have seen. Thank you, Doctor, for explaining the miracle to us. Others might have just called us dumb and laughed at us, but you have been kind and treated our friend with the same care as you do others. We will tell our people and they will know you have come to help us."

One by one, they took the doctor's hand, bowed their thanks and bid goodby. They promised to return the next week to help the man return home and to pay what they could on his bill.

A few days later, Cloyd Stewart came into Ometepec and stopped to see us. We had met the Stewarts in Mexico at the Wycliffe Bible Institute. They worked about eight hours by trail up in the Amusgo Indian country. They had been among the several people who had told us that Ometepec needed a hospital. They also had five children so, naturally, our families had become friends.

Cloyd and his wife, Ruth, had both been through Ometepec several times since we had moved in and they usually stopped by to see us. This time, Cloyd came with his customary warm greeting. Then, with a smile, he added, "And a special congratulation to the doctor who can take pictures below the skin." He had heard about the wonderful treatment the doctor had given the Indian who had been ambushed, and wanted to let us know that the doctor was the talk of the town up in Amusgo country. Jim took Cloyd to see the man and was glad to have someone to explain the medical orders he wanted the man to take back home.

About the time we went to Ometepec, the Government had put in a network of telephones from the telegraph offices in the outlying villages to the telegraph office in Ometepec. This was used for both emergencies and for aiding the Army in keeping peace in the region. Quite often, Jim would receive a notice to go to the telegraph office to receive a call from some village about a serious case.

Cloyd Stewart was a linguist. However, because he had medical supplies and knew more about medicine than anyone else in his village, he was called many times for medical advice. When he had a case he knew was far over his ability, he would call Jim on the telephone and they would decide whether the patient should be sent to Ometepec, or whether Jim should fly to Xochistlahuaca.

On one occasion, Cloyd called Jim and said he had a man who had been stabbed in the abdomen and needed to be sutured. "I don't think it's very deep, but he can hardly walk. If you can

come, there are also some other people who need to see a doctor."
Jim gathered together his instruments and medicine and flew up
to the village.

When he arrived, Cloyd had already cleared off his dining
table and prepared it for surgery. The man was lying on the table
and Jim saw immediately that the wound was worse than Cloyd
had thought. He discussed the problem with the man's family
with Cloyd as interpreter.

They did not want the man taken to Ometepec. He might die
there and they would not be able to bury him in his own village.
The doctor should operate and try to save him. Cloyd could be his
assistant and nurse. Not knowing what was truly involved, the
family had total confidence in the two doctors.

So, there on the dining table in a remote village with only
sleeping pills and local anesthesia for pain, Jim performed major
surgery. He left some penicillin and something for pain with
Cloyd. After a prayer with the Stewarts he returned to Ometepec.

Cloyd called several times to report on the patient. In
spite of everything, he recovered beautifully. No complications,
not even much fever.

He leadeth me! O blessed tho't
O words with heav'nly comfort fraught!
What-e'er I do, wher-e'er I be,
Still 'tis God's hand that leadeth me."

He Leadeth Me, 1st ver.
Joseph H. Gilmore, 1862

Chapter IX

Earthquake!

May and June of 1956 were so busy I wonder how any of us lived through it. We moved into the new house and sorted out what we would take on furlough, what to give away, and what would be stored when we left. I declared that I was in the "throws" of packing: throw it in or throw it out.

Jimmy was finishing eighth grade, Florence sixth, and Peggi third. I should have started Elizabeth in first grade but simply did not have the time for the teacher-supervision first grade requires. Elizabeth already knew her letters and could read beginners' books. Florence had played school with her many times and Florence was a born teacher. I would let her play at school this year and make it up later.

In school, the children had studied U. S. geography and I had combined geography and writing by having them write to the Chamber of Commerce in several large cities, asking for material about their Counties. The responses and the National Geographic Magazines made Jimmy and Florence want to visit several places in Texas and points west. We were to spend our furlough in the south, so the idea of two or three week's vacation travel began to take shape.

Chavela's time to start her work at the British-American Hospital was several weeks before we were to leave, so we decided to close the clinic and open only an office in one of the almost finished rooms in the planned hospital.

Johnny Wood arrived about a month before we were to leave. Madge was expecting their fourth child and James had told them to send her to Morelia as we had nothing set up for obstetrics in Ometepec. Her due date was about the middle of June and we wanted to leave by the first if at all possible.

We managed somehow to get away and had a wonderful three weeks camping in some of the National Parks as we traveled back across the United States to our home for a year in Decatur, Ga. Jim had written to Grady Hospital in Atlanta and was to study in their children's hospital. Jimmy would be in high school. Florence, Peggi and Elizabeth would attend a very fine school near Mission Haven, where we would be living. There would be several other mission families from other parts of the world in the apartments at Mission Haven and plenty of the children just as new to the school system as ours would be.

Billy would be in preschool three days a week. And it was soon pointed out to me that my role would be that of representing the family at school functions, our mission work at various church meetings, keeping the family in clean clothes and well fed, and answering the telephone. In Ometepec, we had not had a telephone and I was amazed at the amount of socializing that people did by phone.

On weekends, we visited many churches and spoke on the work in Ometepec. At the Sardis Presbyterian Church in Charlotte, N.C. (a church with many of Jim's relatives), the men of the church decided to gather a truck load of medical supplies and hospital equipment to send to Mexico when we returned.

In Columbus, Ga., a man who had a hobby of making telescopes was very interested in the story of the eclipse and offered to make us a telescope set at the right degrees for Ometepec. We could use it to teach young people about the stars and moon. He would add it to medical equipment they would collect in Columbus and send down on the truck from Charlotte.

The interest of so many people and the enthusiasm shown in the spiritual and educational opportunities in our neighboring country was very encouraging to us. We knew we should return to finish the job of building the hospital, but the thought of leaving two children in the states weighed heavily on my heart.

Then, one Sunday after church, I met Dr. James Ross McCain, President of Agnes Scott College, and father of Louise Boyce, the relative who had offered to keep Jimmy and Florence when we returned to Mexico. He greeted me with a big smile and exclaimed, "I hear you are going to leave your children with Gene and Louise when you go back to Ometepec. I think that is wonderful."

We talked and he assured me that the children would receive the very best educational opportunities as well as excellent Christian values. I was suddenly filled with a great peace and knew in my heart that God had worked this out also.

Jimmy and Florence had both been studying music while in Decatur; Jimmy both piano and trumpet, and Florence piano. Both wanted to go to Music Camp at Florida State University that summer, so things were really working out for all of us. Florence added violin to her piano lessons that summer.

As soon as school was out, we packed for Florida, summer camp, the trip back to Ometepec, and the beginning of another stage of life in Ometepec. We received word that Chavela was to be married, so she would not be going back with us. I was heartbroken to hear she would not be with us, but not at all surprised at the reason.

Through our mission school of nursing in Morelia, steps were started for student nurses to be able to give their year of social service in Ometepec. As with medical students, nurses were required to give a year of social work in some needy place before they could take their professional exam.

In Mexico City, we were told the bridge over the Papagallo River was out and we would not be able to go overland to Ometepec. Jim inquired about plane fare for all the excess baggage we had, and was offered a special rate if we would go by cargo plane from Puebla. The pilot was the same one who flew the regular flight from Oaxaca to Acapulco, so I had no reason to doubt him when he said we could sit up in the cockpit and go with our baggage.

When we were finally taken to the plane, it was too late to back out. Our baggage was on board, but so were several other tons of boxes. Jim and the children scrambled over the boxes and beckoned to me to follow. I was neither dressed to crawl over boxes, nor physically nor mentally prepared. Besides, there was a distinct odor of a fresh pig pen, and my stomach rebelled. The door of the plane was slammed shut and the motors started. I had nothing to hold on to, and no place to sit except on a box. The odor of pig manure increased when the door was closed. In desperation, I began to crawl over boxes. I shouted to Jim to take my purse and string bag I always carried in Mexico, and with his instructions I finally made it to some fresh air coming in at the cockpit.

"This smells as bad as a pig farm," I gasped.

"Well, he has just brought a load of live pigs from Ometepec and is going to bring another on his return flight. That's why we are getting such a good price on this trip," Jim replied.

"Did you know that when you made the deal?" I queried him.

"I didn't know it was pigs," he said, "I only knew he was hauling some special cargo out."

We had wired Johnny how we would be coming, so were not surprised to see him and his jeep truck waiting for us at the airport. We were surprised to see the town band playing their welcome pieces for us. Several people had made a special trip to the airport just to tell us they were glad to have us again in their town. They followed us into town and at the house we found that a group of the church people had cleaned the dirt and dust out and had a welcoming party in progress. Madge and her four boys greeted us with open arms.

People came by all afternoon to say how happy they were that we had returned. Some said they never expected to see us again once we had left. Others told us about sicknesses they had suffered and friends who had died while we were away. We were tired and I wanted to unpack some sheets and towels, but had no chance until after dark.

Mr. Pascoe, the architect, flew in from Mexico City shortly after we did, so he and Jim immediately began to talk about the work to be done the next day. Madge invited us to her house for supper and I finally told someone to close the gate so we could get bathed and cleaned up to go. I was sure I still smelled of pig manure and could stand it no longer.

When we returned that night, I was determined at least to start unpacking. I opened a few boxes and the large suit cases with clean clothes for the next day. I gave each person a flashlight, as the city lights were still turned off at midnight and no one dared take a step after dark without looking for scorpions. At last, we fell exhausted into bed.

About two o'clock in the morning, there was a loud boom and the house began to shake. All the dogs in town started barking, donkeys braying, and roosters crowing. Sounds of breaking glass and falling objects brought us all fully awake. I tried to find my flashlight but it had fallen on the floor. When I tried to sit up, I was immediately knocked back down as the bed heaved up and down with the house. It only lasted a few seconds, then silence.

From the next room came Billy's small voice. "Mommy, why did we wiggle like that?" he called.

"Stay in bed, Billy," I answered, "We had an earthquake and there is glass on the floor. Let Daddy find the flashlight and we'll come to you."

Then a light beam appeared from down the hall where Mr. Pascoe had been sleeping. In his beautiful British accent we heard, "Hello in theh'ah, hello in theh'ah, is everyone all right?"

"O.K. in here," Jim answered as he found his flashlight. With his light, I was able to see my flashlight half way across the room, and soon we had all the children in one room.

Broken glass and cement dust was everywhere. The roof was still in place but, even in the dark, we could see there were cracks in the walls. Some of the workers were sleeping in the basement of the hospital so we all went to check on them. Other lights were appearing all over town and people could be heard calling to each other. None of the workers was injured but some were coughing because of the dust.

Someone went to check on the Wood's household and came back to report that no one was hurt, but several houses on the street to the Wood's were badly damaged. The roof of one house up town had fallen and an elderly woman killed.

As customary, there were several aftershocks. No one wanted to go back to bed. Mr. Pascoe suggested we boil some water and have a spot of tea. We found a broom and a folding table and, at four o'clock, sat down for tea. The children thought it fun, but the adults,after giving thanks that no one on the place was bodily injured, began to wonder how much the damage would cost and how long opening the hospital would be delayed.

As the sun began to rise over the mountain and daylight brought the full extent of damage to our eyes, we once again gave thanks that no one was injured. Mr. Pascoe, having been trained since childhood what to do in case of a quake, had jumped out of bed at the first boom and rushed into the closet. When he went back to his room after daylight he saw that a brick had fallen from the ceiling onto his pillow!

The hospital had cracks between the windows, but two rooms could be used for a day clinic. Mr. Pascoe had to return to Mexico City but left instructions with the "maestro" on the repair work. After he left, we heard over the radio that Mexico City had been badly hit by the earthquake and we wondered how the Pascoe family and other friends there were. Later, Mr. Pascoe told us that he was in Acapulco waiting for his flight when he heard about the damage in the City and tried in vain to call his wife. "That was the longest flight I ever had, and I was a nervous wreck when I finally reached home," he wrote, "but everyone is all right."

People in Ometepec wasted no time in coming to see the doctor. With no nurse, Jim was having a hard time. He refused to see those who merely wanted to report on their health of the past year, and told everyone he was not really prepared to open his office. That, to a sick person, is not a legitimate excuse for not giving an injection or passing out pills. Or, surely, he could write on a piece of paper what they needed and they could buy it up town at the drug store. Poor Jim! He couldn't find the boxes with his instruments, and didn't have time to look for them. Everything in the building was covered with debris from the earthquake, and the sick kept gathering.

Johnny Wood came over to see how things were and immediately began to help. He talked to the people and explained that we had just arrived the day before and with the earthquake on top of that the doctor was truly too busy trying to get set up to see anyone. "But we have been waiting for several days for him to come," some said. "He's a doctor and should see the sick instead of working on the building," or, "We can wait until he finds his instruments," others declared.

Several women came looking for work. They wanted to be my maid, or work for the doctor, just anything. They thought we would be hiring many people to work and they were willing to do anything we wanted them to do. The only trouble was they didn't have any training. Most could not even read or write, but

Jim sent them all to see me. Without any warning, I was the employment office. By afternoon, I was also the receptionist and office manager.

Peggi, Elizabeth and Billy went to the Wood's house to play with their boys. Their house had considerable damage from the earthquake, and the children were told to play outside under the big tropical tree that shaded almost the entire yard. Madge sent word to me that the children were having a wonderful time and she would feed them at noon. She had hired several men to clean out   the broken glass and dirt from the quake and she could use her kitchen.

How we managed the next few days, I do not remember. I only know that we were frustrated many times, annoyed many times, and so tired we were exhausted. We opened the gate to the hospital only to let in the donkeys bringing building material. People wanting to see the doctor would then push or shove in after the animals. Some wanted work, some medicine, and some just to talk.

I hired a young woman the first day to clean the kitchen and unpack the cooking pots and pans. She knew how to cook, but not on the gas stove. I sent her to the market to buy some vegetables and fruit and she was gone three hours. That afternoon I told her I wouldn't need her the next day.

Then one afternoon a woman we had helped when we lived in the "old house" came to see me. She had gone to Acapulco to work in a hotel and had helped cook and clean rooms. She insisted she knew all about how to work for Americans and would stay in Ometepec if I would hire her. She had two children but they could stay with her cousin when they were not in school. She was the best I could do, so I hired her. She was fairly good help for about two months, then she had to return to Acapulco to see how her mother was doing.

We needed a nurse more than anything, and when word came from Mexico City saying they had two girls who could come for six months, we wired them to come immediately. The doctor's office, examining room and waiting room were finished and the operating room would be in working condition for emergency.(One of the girls returned to Mexico City before the six months was up, but Sarita, a classmate of Chavela's, stayed for over twenty years, except for times she had to go home to Oaxaca to check on her aging parents.)

A young woman who lived nearby came asking for work in the clinic. She was clean, quiet and seemed very pleasant, so we hired her to help the two nurses. She was excellent help except for the fact that she could not read or write.

She and two other girls stopped me one day and asked me if I would teach them to read and write. Madge was helping some young people in the afternoons but these girls worked all day and could only come at night. We had acquired several books of the Laubach method of teaching adults to read, so I agreed to teach three nights a week. They were intelligent and wanted to learn and we had a pleasant time in our evening school.

As soon as Juana could barely write, we put her in charge of keeping the patients in line, telling them the doctor would see patients by number, except in case of emergency. Juana was excellent at this job as she knew almost everyone, and was so very nice to the people even when they were rude to her.

The last part of July we received notice that the truck load of equipment for the hospital was about to leave Charlotte, N.C. and would go by way of Columbus, Ga. for the things that had been collected there. Some very good serving trays, kitchen equipment, and operating room furniture had been bought from the Army Surplus Store and, with the telescope, the truck was full. They were traveling with two men in the truck and two in a car, in case of a breakdown in some isolated region.

Jim had told them they would probably have to transfer everything to a Mexican truck at the border, as no U.S.A. trucks were allowed to carry cargo into the interior of Mexico. He had also been to see the Governor of our state to obtain permission to import the equipment.

As communication by mail was slow, we sent several telegrams, instructing the men to meet Jim in Chilpancingo. The men did not receive the telegrams, but were told to leave the things in a storehouse in Brownsville until the import permission arrived. They took what they could in the car and drove nonstop to Acapulco. There they sent a telegram to us saying they were hiring a local pilot to bring them to Ometepec. They would have to fly back that afternoon.

It was a Sunday morning. Jim was waiting for the men in Chilpancingo and even if I sent a telegram he would not be able to get back in time to meet our guests. I sent the telegram just in case another little miracle might happen. I also knew He would be heartbroken if he did not see the men, and that he thought it very important for the men to meet the Governor. (Or for the Governor to meet them, I wasn't sure which was top priority.)

Johnny had to direct Sunday school and church service, but he came by our house on the way. I showed him the telegram and asked his advice. Johnny was very good at working things around schedules and, as church services were not conducted by strict time, he was sure he could work it out. He would direct the services until he heard a small plane circle the city, then turn things over to Don Ramon, an elder in the church. Then he would rush out to the air strip to meet the men. He had practiced this run many times when we lived downtown and was sure the pilot would tell the men he would be right there. The children could go to Sunday school, but I would stay home in case someone in a truck offered our guests a ride before Johnny arrived.

I also added more rice to the casserole, made a larger fruit salad, and made a large pitcher of limeade. I was glad I had made extra bread the day before. I was very glad our kerosene refrigerator was working well and we had plenty of ice.

About one o'clock I heard the plane, and shortly thereafter I heard Johnny's jeep speed by on the main road. The men wanted to see everything: the town, the hospital, the people, and Jim. What possibility was there that they could meet him in Acapulco or Chilpancingo? With no telephone, (The men were surprised there was only a short line connection to a few regional towns), I knew no way to reach Jim, and I had no way of knowing if he had received the message I had sent earlier.

Johnny had returned to the church to bring Madge and the children home and, in his fast forward fashion, had an answer to our problem. "I'll fly back to Acapulco with you and, if necessary, all the way to Chilpancingo. We'll leave word with several friends in Acapulco and maybe we'll make contact. I can be ready to leave in five minutes."

Bode, the local pilot who was taking the men, was a Mayan Indian from Yucatan, but had run a local taxi-plane service for a number of years. He knew no English and had talked to the men by sign language on the way over. Both the visitors and Bode were glad to have Johnny return with them.

About fifteen minutes out of Ometepec, Bode spoke rapidly to Johnny in Spanish: "Look up there! Isn't that Pepe's plane? He has circled around and seems to be signaling something."

"Yes, you're right. Isn't that Doctor Boyce waving to us?"

The men were astonished as the pilots exchanged sign language and Jim joined in.

"There is a landing field right over to our left and they want us to land there,"Johnny translated. "Doctor Boyce says he will go back with you. That's great. I can go back to Ometepec with Pepe and be there for the afternoon service."

The pilots were excellent bush-pilots and soon they were on the ground. They did some quick exchange of passengers and Jim returned to Acapulco with the men from Charlotte. They spent that night in Chilpancingo and the next morning he took them to meet the Governor. The permission to deliver the hospital equipment to Ometepec was presented and the men went happily back to the Border. They took back with them a greater understanding of our two worlds, one with fast cars and roads for them to run on, the other struggling to move from the donkey to the airplane without the intermediate stages of trains or cars. One with many means of communication, the other still depending on personal conversation and hand-shakes to do business. Above all, we have a first-hand example of how the wisdom and power of our God of love can change lives, and the joy we can have when we take part in His kingdom.

When the equipment arrived, it was stored in the basement of the hospital until the patient rooms were completed. Things were beginning to shape up and fall into place, and plans for an official opening in June 1958, were being made.

People from out of town were brought out to see the hospital, especially visitors with families in Ometepec. "We are happy to have you here," many said, "our region has been neglected too long."

Many local people said the maternity ward was not needed and should be planned for something else. "A woman will never go to a man for her delivery," we heard many times. Nevertheless, the labor and delivery rooms were finished the same time as the operating room. When people told Jim he was wasting space and money, he would merely smile and say, "We'll see, we'll see."

In May 1958, there was a terrible wreck in San Juan de los Llanos, about fourteen kilometers down the mountain from Ometepec. Without any advance notice, the wounded were delivered to our hospital in Ometepec. We had no beds up, no nurse (Sarita was taking time to check on her mother before we officially opened the hospital), no working kitchen, one doctor and nine badly wounded patients.

There was also a crowd of shouting, crying people pouring into the hospital to see if any of the wounded were of their family. Johnny and Madge came rushing over to help and our friend,Jack McClendon from Teloloapan, happened to be visiting. I was even called to help and, in spite of my queazy stomach, managed to work all afternoon without losing control.

Madge and Jack were very good nurses, and Jim asked Jack to help him in the operating room. Johnny took charge of the crowd and finally had only the immediate families of wounded inside the hospital. The Government health control doctor had to be notified and only first aid could be administered before he arrived. Surprisingly, he did not delay, and after declaring this a major accident on the new highway, he saw his job finished, and left.

One man had massive internal injuries and died fifteen minutes after arriving. He had bled from the time of the accident until he was placed on a cot in the waiting room. When Jim rushed to see him, the patient was unconscious. He was not from Ometepec and a messenger was sent uptown to notify the town President. We didn't even know his name, nor where he was from.

One by one, the patients were taken to the operating room where Jim and Jack sewed, bandaged and put on casts as fast as they could. They took the patients in order of the seriousness of their wounds, and some were truly serious. Some needed blood transfusions, but there was no blood. We already knew the people had almost a mortal fear of giving blood, a fetish seemingly going back to the ancient Aztec times. Jim did have several bottles of glucose on hand, and used them all before the day was over.

One man, left to the last, had both legs broken above the

knees. He did not complain very much, but said he was thankful he was not as bad as the others. He had been riding on top of the truck that skidded on the ramp up to the new bridge. As usual, the truck was carrying cargo and passengers. Most of the cargo was large bags of corn and this man was riding on top of the corn. When the truck skidded down the embankment, he was thrown to one side and two bags of corn landed across his legs. He was pinned there for several minutes while people rushed to uncover the other victims.

This man was from the coastal village of San Nicolas, a Black village. He had no family near and told us he didn't know when they would know about him. He had been on the way to find work in Acapulco. Maybe someone would notify them that he was on that truck. Late in the afternoon, he told me he was hungry for there had been nothing to eat since early morning.

I suddenly realized that no one had eaten anything since morning, and I had no idea if or what they could eat. When they rolled the next person out of the operation room, I quickly asked Jim what we should do about the hungry people.

"See what you have at home. Jello, if you have some, tea, coffee, and Pepsi. Some can have more as they have no internal injuries. Tell those we haven't seen yet to please wait until after I exam them. They can have a little Pepsi. See what you can find and I'll tell you what each one can have when we finish in the operating room."

Johnny had been putting up beds in some unfinished rooms and helping transfer patients from the waiting room to patient rooms and in and out of the operating room. He and Madge and I had a conference on food and I went over to our house to see what I could find. We had used all our ice in making ice bags for bruises, so I couldn't make quick Jello. Our children all liked a drink made out of Jello and lime juice. They would drink it warm, and knowing that the Mexicans did not drink anything cold when ill, I decided to try it. Two or three church women had come to see if they could help and I asked one to make "atole de arroz" (a thin milk,rice and cinnamon drink.) I gave another some money to go look for sweet bread.

By the time they finished in the operating room, all who were able to eat had a tray ready. Two or three had intravenous fluids, and two or three didn't want anything except Pepsi. The family members by their beds asked if they could have what was left on the tray. They, too, were hungry, and most lived a long way from Ometepec. We fed people until the food gave out, then started cleaning up the waiting room.

Except for the one man who died before the doctor could get to him, the patients recovered rather rapidly. The man with both legs broken did have family come to see him. But when they saw him in the cast, they said they could not get him on a horse so would have to leave him with us. Most patients left after a week but Rafael stayed six weeks.

Whether we were ready or not, our hospital was unofficially opened two months before the set date. I quickly hired a cook and someone to run errands for her. The hospital kitchen was placed second to operating room in priority.

The Governor had been asked to speak at the inauguration and had accepted. Several people were coming from the States and we planned for two big days of celebration. Saturday would be for the civil and professional requirements, then Sunday for the religious ceremonies at the church service.

The Amusgo choir from up in the Indian territory offered to sing and we were delighted with their offer. Amy Buaurnsmidt, a nurse, and Marjorie Buck, a linguist, had joined the Wycliffe Bible Translators about the time we came to Ometepec. They had been sent to work with the Stewarts in Xochistlahuaca. Amy also taught their church choirs. Their language was tonal so the music had to be adapted to fit the words.

The day before the big date, the men who were to make the barbecue came to report that three of the goats brought in were absolutely too thin to kill. "All bones, no meat," they said.

We had a conference and sent two men off to find some suitable goats. The women came to set up their stands for the making of tortillas, Johnny hauled chairs from the church and his house, and our children carried over all we did not need for breakfast the next morning.

Late in the afternoon, a telegram arrived saying that the plane flight scheduled to bring the visitors from the States had been cancelled because of bad weather. They would go to Acapulco and try to get a flight from there. Among those coming were

Paula West, an R.N. with a degree in Religious Education, and four nurses from Morelia, assigned to do social service for a year in our hospital. Paula could only stay two days but would be back as soon as she finished her language studies.

Early on the morning of the big event, a telegram from Chilpancingo informed us that the Governor could not make it. We were beginning to wonder what we would do for a program. Two hours before the time to begin, a plane from Acapulco did bring our visitors from Morelia and the States. Dr. Hervey Ross was their guide and we were glad they had made connections.

Jim was called to the hospital to see a school teacher he had been seeing for prenatal care for about three months. She was married to another school teacher and knew about prenatal care. It didn't take Jim long to see the baby was coming that day, and probably that morning.

He called Dr. Ross and they decided that Johnny and Dr. Ross would take care of the program and Jim would deliver the first baby to be born in a hospital in Ometepec. One of the visitors set up his recorder to record the first cry. The program started only one hour late.

At the close of the program, Jim came in and played the recording of the baby's first cry and the mother's first words, "Thanks be to God." Everyone applauded and declared that to be a very appropriate inauguration of the hospital. Madge had made a beautiful plaque to be unveiled and everyone was pleased with its message:

Sanatorio de la Amistad
Dedicado a la Gloria de Dios
Y el servicio a la humanidad
Junio 28, 1958

(Friendship Hospital, dedicated to the Glory of God and the service of mankind. June 28, 1958.) The name "Friendship Hospital" had been selected by the youth of the Presbyterian Church, U.S. at their national conference in Montreat, North Carolina the summer of 1956.

We almost didn't have enough barbecue. Madge and I and the others serving watched the last bit eaten by people who had already had too much, but we enjoyed our tortillas covered with the sauce.

The next day's services were very well done and our little church was overflowing with people from far and near. By Monday morning all the visitors had left, some walking, some riding their donkeys, and some in airplanes.

Friendship Hospital had finally been officially inaugurated.

"God moves in a mysterious way
His wonders to perform;
He plants His footsteps in the sea
and rides upon the storm."

God Moves in a Mysterious Way
William Cowper, 1774

Chapter X

Easter and Ancient Spring Rituals

The summer of 1958 was an exciting one for all of us. Jimmy and Florence had returned for their vacation and several other friends came from the U.S. to see the new hospital. Paula West, our new director of nurses, finished her language course and we welcomed her with much joy. I was delighted to turn everything pertaining to nursing over to her. Morelia had also sent three graduate nurses to do their social service in Ometepec.

During the summer, Jimmy and Nacho had spent many hours in the evening with the telescope brought from Columbus, Georgia. They studied maps of stars and moon and looked at them through the new machine. By the time Jimmy had to leave, Nacho had learned to set up and adjust the telescope. They had invited several of the boys from the secondary school to join them, and all were fascinated with what they saw. Nacho asked permission to use the telescope for a school project and we were glad for him to do so.

A new anesthesia machine had been bought by the Decatur Presbyterian Church and Paula had studied in Morelia how to use it. We had taken a short vacation in August to return our children to Tallahassee and Jim had made some more purchases on the way back.

When we arrived in Ometepec, three very serious patients were waiting for Jim. So were some very anxious nurses. That night, the new anesthesia machine was used and Paula and Jim began a new era of surgical care in southern Mexico.

Two days later, as the doctor was dressing the wound the man said, "Oh, Doctor, what divine hands you have!"

"No, Senor, my hands are not divine," Jim replied.

"Well, God is certainly blessing your hands, for you are doing wonderful things here."

"Yes, you are right there," Jim said, "Whatever I do, I ask God's help, and in your case especially, we can say God blessed in a wonderful way. We must give Him the thanks."

One day a group of people brought a woman in a hammock. She had been in labor for three days and the midwives had done all they knew how to do. One said to Jim, "Now see what you can do!" With that, most of the people left.

The baby was already dead and the mother in very serious condition. With the skill of doctor and nurses, the mother's life

Paula West: nurse, anesthesiologist, Christian Educator. Served Hospital de la Amistad from 1958—1972.

was saved. "Next time," Jim told her, "come in for prenatal care and you can have a live baby."

To encourage the expectant mothers to come in for prenatal care, we did not charge anything until delivery, and the price of that was lowered to the price of the midwives. One mother of a very prominent family brought her pregnant daughter to see the hospital and talk to the nurses about the care given the patients. "I lost three babies at childbirth," she declared. "If there had been this kind of hospital then, I would not have lost them."

A few months later this young mother had her baby in our

hospital and the grandmother announced to everyone she knew that all women should go to the hospital to have their babies. Soon the maternity ward was filling up.   Many nights, Jim and/or the nurses had little sleep.

In the old house downtown, our friend with the pine knot torch had often come to call the doctor at night. Now we had the night watchman who would knock on our window and proclaim: "Doctor, a wounded person," or "Doctor, a delivery."

In order to have a Registered Nurse degree, the students had to be able to deliver a baby, and to know when to call a doctor in case of trouble. Sarita had her degree in Midwifery, and was excellent in teaching the girls when to call the doctor. Sarita and Chavela had both been trained under Dr. Marroquin in Mexico City, and had been well trained in showing love as well as teaching it. We missed Chavela, but were glad we had Sarita to take her place.

Teaching the cooks how to prepare food on a gas stove, and what to prepare for a liquid, soft or regular diet, was not hard, but we couldn't keep the young people after they had learned. I asked a few questions and discovered that as soon as the cooks thought they knew enough, they would go to Acapulco to look for a higher paying job in a hotel. They would claim to have learned to cook in an American home and knew what tourists would like to eat. I don't know how many kept their jobs. I had never taught them anything except plain cooking.

However, I was getting provoked with losing so many cooks just when I thought I could turn things over to them. I told Jim I was going to find an older woman with a large family and see if she would stay in Ometepec. He discovered that Antonia, a woman we had hired several months before to clean floors was a widow with seven girls, and he told me to talk to her. She was a hard worker and probably would like to make more money.

So Dona Antonia entered our staff. She was the hardest worker I had ever seen. In fact, I had to tell her not to come at four o'clock in the morning. At this hour, she seemed to think everyone, including the patients, should be awake. She bustled about the kitchen boiling water, sterilizing baby bottles and making cinnamon tea for the new born babies. The girls who worked for her complained that she was too strict, and that she insisted everything be done exactly as I had taught her. I was thankful I had at last found someone I could depend on to do the work and to stay in Ometepec. The nurses found out they could either complain to Paula or me and we would try to work things out.

One morning, Dona Antonia came to me very early and asked, with a twinkle in her eyes: "Senora, what do I prepare for the dead boy?"

I must have looked surprised, for I really wondered if I had heard right, "Who?" I asked.

"You remember the boy they brought in from a village last week? He had been in a fight and ran to a neighbor's house and collapsed. They thought he was dead and even had him prepared for the funeral, with candles all around him, when somebody noticed a twitch in one eye. They blew out the candles and brought him in here. He was unconscious but his heart was still beating. Well, last night he awoke and said 'Mama'."

When Jim came over for breakfast he,too, was excited about the boy. "He also declared he was hungry," Jim added with a smile."He'll be able to go home in a few days."

As Easter approached, Johnny said he thought we all ought to go to Igualapa for their big fiesta four .weeks before Easter. We had heard much about this event in the years we had lived in Ometepec, but had never ventured over the mountain to the little town. For one thing, it was a rough trail and a jeep could barely make it. Most people walked or rode a donkey. Merchants going to sell their wares walked and drove their donkeys loaded down with whatever they were planning to sell. The variety was amazing.

Everything from stockings and jewelry to cooking pans and soap. Three tribes of Indians gathered to have their tribal dances in the church yard. They passed through Ometepec in groups for several days before the ceremony was to begin.

We had been told that this town was where the Indians had worshipped their rain god before the Spaniards arrived. Women told me that the Indian women, in years past, would wear only long straight skirts, with no tops. The men would gather along the street and whistle and laugh as they went by. Then the government sent some merchants in with bibbed aprons and convinced the Indians that this, over the skirts, was the proper thing to wear. Now the men don't gather to watch them go by.

I was interested in learning about their pilgrimage and dances to the rain god, so I went to talk to Don Ramon and his wife. Don Ramon was quite a historian and an interesting story teller. His family had lived in Ometepec for generations and had passed the history down by word of mouth. This was his story: "Before the Spaniards arrived in the early seventeenth century, Igualapa had been a religious center for the Aztecs. Three tribes gathered there every spring to celebrate the beginning of the rainy season. It was said (but not verified) that they made sacrifices to the gods and dropped the blood from a certain height onto a large rock below. If the blood splashed in a big circle, it meant they would have a good rainy season and could plant corn early. If it barely splashed, they could expect a drought. The dances were before the ceremonies and were a form of worship so the god would hear them when they made their sacrifice.

When the Spaniards arrived, they did in Igualapa what they had done in the northern part of Mexico. They looked for the religious centers of the Indians and built Catholic churches over the most holy grounds. The Indians would always return to their sacred spot for their services, so they became Catholics in part, but would continue their old religious ceremonies in the church yard. They attend mass in the church and have their dances in the church yard. Some people say they go into the hills and have a secret ceremony, where a chicken is killed and held over a large rock. They still want to know if they will have a good rainy season or not."

We had all talked about going to the fiesta someday and Johnny said he had reports that the road was very much improved. We could leave early on Friday, take a lunch and return before dark. Few people would be looking for the doctor on that day as it was reported they were bringing a saint from Mexico City who would perform miracles and all sick people should go. We weren't sick, but we were curious. So we left Sarita in charge at the hospital and crowded into the jeep truck.

It was one of those trips where I can truthfully say I am glad I went, but hope and pray I will never again have to make.

They had indeed worked on the road in places. Some of these places were worse than where they had not tried to improve.

Going over we were behind donkey trains much of the time and could go along only as fast as they were going. Sometimes the drivers of the donkeys would send them single file next to the mountain and let us pass. At the streams, we would all get out of the truck and wade across, hoping the lighter load would not get stuck.

Just before we came to the town, we passed a huge fenced in corral with more donkeys in it than we had ever seen in one place. Their brays were like a wild symphony. They all seemed to bray at the same time. We stopped to look and laugh and again wondered how the ancient tribes of Indians ever found this place to worship. We stopped again at the top of the last mountain to admire in awe the breath taking view. We understood a little better why they would be compelled to worship a higher being. We, too, felt a mightier hand than ours and sang This is My Father's World.

An airplane flew over high up in the skies and disappeared over the distant mountain. The donkeys reminded us that there are many people in the world who have not learned of airplanes, trains and automobiles. "Go into all the world'" Christ told His followers. "Teach, heal, baptize."

The fiesta was at its peak, and the sun was getting hot before we reached the center of town. Our vehicle had been required to stop on the outskirts of town, so we had to carry our lunch and water with us. I'm sure we looked as strange to those people as they did to us, but Johnny and Jim were recognized by many at the fiesta. We really wanted to see the dances in the church yard, but were told they would not start until the sun was a little cooler.

When one of the Indians saw our disappointment, he said he would see if they could have the first dance at four o'clock. So we waited, thinking that we could go down the mountain faster than climb up. What we didn't realize was that the last mass was said at three o'clock and then there would be a great exodus of people, donkeys, jeeps, and trucks and the one lane road would be full to overflowing. It was after dark when we arrived home, but we all felt the Indian dances were worth waiting to see, and the whole trip worth our aching bones the next day.

As Easter was approaching, everyone was preparing for the big town celebration or the church programs. Johnny and Madge were training a choir and planning to have an Easter sunrise service in their front yard. It had a beautiful view, just as Madge had thought it would be when she picked that place. Ometepec lay in all its unique beauty on a hill lower than the Wood's house.

One day an elderly patient was talking to me about Captain Brenton. She mentioned that he walked up to that tree every day he could and sat for hours.

"That tree in the Wood's yard?" I asked with much interest.

"That very tree," she said. "Dona Rachel lived on Main Street at the top of that trail," she said, pointing to the trail leading from the Wood's house up town. "Captain Brenton walked slowly because he was very weak, but he liked to sit under that tree."

I could hardly wait to tell Madge, for we had read many times the passages in the Captain's Bible where he had prayed for missionary families to be sent to Ometepec. Now, years after his death, that prayer had been answered.

The week before Easter week, Nacho asked for permission to borrow the telescope again. The science club in school needed money and they were trying to think of ways to earn some. If it could be done by a means of teaching something related to science, all the better. As there is always a full moon during Easter week, they thought it would be a great thing to set up the telescope each night and let people look at the moon for twenty centavos a look. (At that time twenty centavos was less than two cents.) Nacho would be responsible for the telescope, but he had two other boys who also knew how to focus and instruct others in what they would see.

When we said they could use the telescope, they rushed up town to ask the town council for permission to use the open place in front of the school. Nacho reported to us that the lines were long every night and many people came back several times to see the moon. Some people were skeptical, some afraid, but the young people were fascinated.

The Easter service was a splendid, inspiring event. The sun sent its pink rays over the tallest mountain just as the program started. It was several minutes before it arose in full force, but the few clouds in the sky made an inspring backdrop for the Easter announcement: "Christ Arose. Halleluia!"

Jim was still visiting several towns along the coastal plains and Johnny went with him most of the time. Johnny would finish his Bible classes long before Jim would finish with the sick. Also they both needed help. Jim needed a nurse to give out medicinal instructions and to help with small children. Johnny needed someone to teach the small children while he taught the adults. Jims' Piper Cub would only carry two passengers, so Johnny learned to fly and bought his own plane.

Madge prepared children's classes and handwork for fifty or more children three or four times a week. With her own children to teach, she didn't have time to go with Johnny, so the mission sent a young graduate of the National Bible School to help Johnny.

On Monday after Easter, a trucker stopped at the hospital to talk to the Doctor. An old man had been abandoned on someone's steps on Saturday night. He was very ill, was not conscious, and seemed to have a high fever. If they would bring him to the hospital, would the doctor treat him? He smelled bad, was dirty, ragged, and would probably die, but some of the people in town thought it was terrible just to let him die without even trying to do anything. So this trucker offered to come see if the Doctor would take the case.

"We never turn down anyone," Jim told him, "So bring him in."

I happened to be in the hospital when they returned with the man, and to say he smelled bad was truly an understatement. They carried him down the hall to a private room where Paula and another nurse began the terrible job of cleaning him up.

"Marguerite, can you get us some crushed ice?" Paula called from the man's door.

The kitchen was out of ice, so I rushed over to our house to get some. How sweet the fresh air was! I didn't stop to smell the roses, but I was thankful for the few fresh breaths of air I had before rushing back with the ice.

How fast those nurses worked! They had already discarded his clothes and were in the last stages of bathing the patient.

"Could you please spoon a little ice into his mouth?" Paula asked, "He is very dehydrated. Doctor says he thinks the old man has typhoid, plus other things."

I stood giving the man small sips of crushed ice while the

two nurses put a hospital gown on him. Suddenly, he grabbed my arm and exclaimed: "Where am I? Tell me, where am I? Am I in heaven?" With that he sank back into unconsciousness.

"Paula, you and Anita, dressed in white, throwing a large white sheet over him, probably did make him think he was in heaven." I said with a smile.

The old man was in the hospital several days, sometimes conscious. The nurses said he talked sometimes but they couldn't understand what he said. He kept calling for Guadalupe. Guadalupe is the patron saint of Mexico, and also the name of many people, so the nurses would ask, "Guadalupe, who?" and he would just repeat the name again.

In the meantime, everyone in town was trying to find out where the old man lived and who had abandoned him. He had been carried in on a very worn out, filthy hammock so had evidently come a long distance.

With medical care and food, the man was able to tell us his name in about ten days. He had indeed traveled a long way. They were on their way to Igualapa to ask the saint they had heard would be there, to cure him. As they reached the outskirts of Ometepec, they realized they could not make it to Igualapa in time for the fiesta. He had told the men to return home. He didn't think he could make the trip back. That was all he remembered.

He gave us the name of his town and said his son was named Guadalupe. It took over a month to get in touch with his son, then he didn't believe the message. Finally, General Monroe was asked if he could send word through his army connections for the son to come take his father home.

In the meantime, the man asked to go to the morning devotional. He had heard the singing and wanted to know about this God of Love. He had called Jim and the nurses saints several times, and Paula had teased him about thinking he was in heaven when he first saw them. The man could read, and asked for a Bible. When his son finally arrived, the old man walked out of the hospital carrying his Bible tucked under his arm.

Up in Xochistlahuaca, a group of Indians met twice a week to read and study the Bible as the Wycliffe workers translated it. First, they had to learn to read and Amy had written readers for this purpose. They were taught in Amusgo, a language that had never even been in written form. Most of the Indians did not even know Spanish, so it was truly starting out in simplest form.

Those who were learning Biblical truths wanted their children to go to school, but the only school was limited to first and second grades and was taught in Spanish. So one Sunday a group of the leaders of the congregation in Xochistlahuaca came to Ometepec and asked if some of the members of the congregation would consider taking some of the Indian children to live with them during the school year so they could attend school. The children would work for their board and keep. And if they ever gave any trouble, the parent would immediately come to get the trouble maker.

Two of our children were already in the States and Peggi would be leaving soon. Naturally, I thought: if Gene and Louise Boyce can take in three of our children, surely we can open our home to three of these children. Madge and Johnny had already told a girl from a different town she could live with them. Nacho would be leaving soon to go to Mexico City to attend preparatory school. We agreed to take in two girls and one boy.

The boy was Billy's roommate; the girls moved in with Elizabeth. The first night I heard Carlos cough all night long. The next morning I asked him how long he had had a cough, and he said he didn't know, but maybe several weeks.

That afternoon Jim took Carlos to the hospital to x-ray his chest and make some other tests. "Carlos has tuberculosis," he told me that night. " We must get in touch with his father to get permission to treat him." Two days later the father came in bringing two other children with him. They, too, had coughs and if the doctor would be so kind as to treat all of them, the family would be very grateful.

Jim questioned him about the family and discovered the parents and eight children slept in the same room on two or three straw mats. They did not have sufficient food and could not afford a proper diet. He had me write a letter to Amy explaining what he had found, and asked her to see to it that all the children received the medicine he was sending with the father. Carlos stayed with us and with a good diet and new medicines, he was soon on the way to recovery.

Several months later, his father came to thank the Doctor.

With tears in his eyes, he said in broken Spanish, "Oh, Doctor, if God had not sent you to this town, all of my children could have died. I do not have money to pay you, but I will pray for you every day. I pray that God will repay you."

Ever since Jim treated his first patient with leprosy, he had been receiving requests to please go to this ranch, or someone's isolated home, to see a patient who could not come into Ometepec. The requests were made by family members, some of whom would not even say what the symptoms were, nor give any history of the case.

"We don't know what he has," they would tell the Doctor. "But we know you will be able to tell us and give us medicine." Sometimes a hint was given by saying it was a "bad" disease. In five years his file on leprosy had grown to almost one hundred patients, and word began to spread that he really did have a medicine that would stop this dreaded illness. The American Mission to Lepers always kept Jim supplied with sufficient medicine.

One afternoon Jim was called to the telegraph office to receive two telephone calls. One was from Johnny who had gone to a village in the jeep truck. They had a flat and needed something from his tool chest. He wanted Jim to send one of the workmen out with it so they could get back before dark. The other call was from Amy in Indian country and about all Jim could hear was, "We need you, please come."

Sometimes the lines would become twisted and somehow three people could talk at once and this was one of those times. The conversation went something like this:

Johnny: "Jim, tell Catarino to bring the tool box immediately."

Amy: "Doctor, we need you. Emergency."

Jim: "I can't hear either one. What's the emergency?"

Johnny: "We can't get the tire off."

Amy: "I can't hear you. Doctor, we need you."

Jim: "Where is the tool box?"

Amy: "Doctor, please come to Xochistlahuaca."

Johnny: "I'm in Santa Maria. Tell Catarino to get a horse and hurry."

A few minutes later, Jim came hurrying in the house. "I hope I got all that garbled talk straight. Johnny wants his tool box to get a tire off and Amy wants me for some emergency which I could not hear because Johnny's voice was nearer. He wants his tool box. I hope it's not Amy that needs a tool box and Johnny that needs a doctor. That line is almost good for nothing sometimes." Yet we were thankful for the little connections we had.

When Jim landed in Xochistlahuaca one of the struts on the plane doubled under the plane. He was very upset but went on to see the patient Amy had called him to see. He sent Cloyd to call Ometepec and ask one of the taxi pilots to come for him.

Bode came and they looked the plane over. "It looks like metal fatigue to me," Bodi said." I'm going to Chilpancingo tomorrow and I'll ask Barcenas to come if you want me to."

Barcenas was an excellent mechanic and a good friend, and Jim did indeed want him. It was several weeks before the plane was back in commission. Barcenas was still a little doubtful about several pieces of metal.

In the fall of 1960, we went to Tallahassee to see the two children there and also to leave Peggi to attend High School. Peggi did not want to leave Ometepec and we both cried several times on the way.

While in Tallahassee, Jim visited a number of minister friends, and especially wanted to visit Bill Cristie, because he was making a plane in his basement. The two men became lifelong friends, with interests in flying and spreading the gospel of the God of Love.

We enjoyed visiting with our children and seeing how they had grown in body, mind, and spirit. Louise said they did all right socially, also. I hated to leave them, but again I knew it was the thing to do.

Soon after we returned to Ometepec, we received a letter from Bill Cristie telling us that he and his wife had a great idea: at least, they thought so. This was the time of Green Stamps in the United States, and they wondered what we would think if they started a campaign to buy a new airplane to replace "The Messenger". He had written the Board for permission and they had given it. Bill didn't know how many stamps it would take, but they wanted our permission to go ahead and try this unusual project.

We had not lived in the States long enough to realize the

extent of this "Green Stamp Mania", but were glad to let them try. Mrs. Christie, a faithful worker in the Women of the Church, suggested they appeal to the women to sponsor the idea. This was an excellent idea, as it was the women who collected most of the stamps. The Christies wrote to our supporting churches and all of them entered the project with enthusiasm. Mrs. Christie and her children offered to stick the stamps in the books. (All of them declared they had very green fingers as well as thumbs before they finished.) Five million Green Stamps would be required. It would take about a year or year and a half to complete the project.

Nineteen sixty-one started off with many activities planned for the year. The Woods were to go on furlough in June and Johnny wanted to do a years work in six months. He lacked personnel, however, as Nacho was now attending the Seminary in Mexico City. Two other men attended Bible School and one was back to help. He was not as quick to understand as Nacho, neither was he as reliable. Johnny was therefore very happy when Nacho said he could return to Ometepec once or twice a month to help with the church services.

There was also another reason for his returning, but we were

John and Madge with their five sons leaving for furlough in 1961.

too busy to realize it. Madge took me aside one day and asked me if I had noticed that Nacho seemed interested in one of our nurses. I had not, but you can be sure I started paying attention.

A few days later I cornered Madge and asked, "Were you trying to tell me that Nacho and Maria are dating? Is that one reason he is coming back? Would that be one influence in her decision to stay another year after she finished her social service?"

When Jim heard about it he said, "Well, I hope they don't marry until we can find a replacement for Maria. She is one of our best nurses!"

Love won out in this case, though. Johnny and Madge arranged to be witnesses at the marriage of Nacho and Maria just before leaving on furlough. Maria was soon hired at the British American Hospital and worked until Nacho finished Seminary.

> Saviour, like a Shepherd lead us,
> Much we need Thy tender care;
> In Thy pleasant pastures feed us,
> For our use Thy folds prepare:
> Blessed Jesus, Blessed Jesus,
> Thou hast bought us, Thine we are.

> *Savior, Like a Shepherd Lead Us.*
> Dorothy A. Thrupp, 1836

Chapter XI

Women and Green Stamps

One of the plans Don Ramon was enthusiastically sponsoring was the dedication of a monument at the grave site of Captain Brenton. Don Ramon had not read the Captain's Bible the thirty years he had kept it before we went to Ometepec, but he was earnestly reading the new Bible we gave him. He also read the Mexican History of the formation of the first Frigate School. He was amazed at the Captain's part in Mexican history. "He was a great man in history, and we must place a marker on his grave." Don Ramon talked to everyone about his idea. Senor Pascoe, the architect, was the grandson of a British missionary who had married a Mexican woman. He was also the son of the first Mexican Methodist Bishop in Mexico. Don Ramon's enthusiasm spilled over to all of us and we began to present the idea to the National Presbyterian Church.

The plan for the monument was designed. It would hold a torch with an open Bible underneath. The Bible would have the words taken from the Captain's Bible: "The Entrance of Thy Word Giveth Light." There would also be a plaque with a short record of his naval career. In order to use these words, someone had to ask permission from the head of the Mexican Naval Department. Don Ramon asked Jim to go by the Naval office when we were on one of our business trips to the City. Jim had a little doubt about an American asking the favor, however, he finally agreed to do so.

The Head of the Naval Department was an elderly man and when Jim stated his request, the Officer became very excited. "Did you know Captain Brenton?" he asked.

"No, Sir," Jim replied," but I know where he was buried and

some people in that small town want to place a marker on his grave."

"He was called the 'Father' of our Navy," the officer said. "And we did not know when nor where he died. You send me the exact words you want to use, and I will take it to the President of Mexico for his approval."

On May 24, 1962, the Monument to Brigadier Carey Brenton was unveiled in the Ometepec graveyard. The British Embassy sent a flag to be used in the service. The Mexican Navy sent a corps of Marines to stand guard during the ceremony. The principal speaker was Senor Juan Pascoe, father of the architect of our hospital. The schools were ordered to study about the famous Naval Officer buried in Ometepec. They made wreathes to carry to the cemetery. The service in the church the next day was dedicated to the religious services Captain Brenton had rendered in Mexico. In his last years, he had walked hundreds of miles selling Bibles and calling on people to start house churches with Bible study and prayer.

Don Ramon was eloquent when he said: "God sent one man to sow the seed, and look what is being harvested today. Captain Brenton prayed for us. We must pray and learn about God's Word so that we can pass on the torch. This week we have honored the man who came to give us the light of God's Word."

The bronze plaque on the monument said simply:
Captain R. Carey Brenton
Brigadier de la Marina National Mexicana
y Real Marina Britanica.
Diciembre 22 de 1848-Abril 18, 1921
Un siervo de Dios y de los hombres
Dejo su Tierra Natal para dedicar
su vida a Mexico

(Captain R. Carey Brenton, Brigadier of the National Mexican Navy and the Royal British Marines, December 22, 1848-April 18, 1921, A Servant of God and of Man. He left his native land to dedicate his life to Mexico.)

The hospital was growing faster than we could find competent workers. More and more I was called on to help out in the drug store. I was given some more "on the job" training when we bought a new cash register. It had several buttons to help keep the funds separated according to departments. "In patient" and "out patient" accounts must be kept separate. So should the operating room be separate from the clinic records. It complicated the bookkeeping, but the Mission business expert said it was necessary. Paula and I spent hours at night trying to make everything balance. Neither of us had any bookkeeping experience, but it fell on us to learn.

When the Woods went on furlough the Mission sent a new missionary couple to live in their house and to help in the work of the church. Mr. Floyd Bishop, a Missionary Aviation Fellowship pilot, came to fly the missionary to the villages in which Johnny had started work on a regular schedule.The Bishops had a son Billy's age and the two soon became good friends.

Jim had some strange cases that year. Donkey bites, snake bites, and anxiety attacks caused by someone having broken some "voo-doo" spell. One such case had Jim puzzled for a day or two. He went back to his medical books several times to look up symptoms. Then he realized the man was not consistent in his answers, and he began to ask more detailed questions. Finally the man exclaimed: "Doctor, I'll tell you what happened. Two weeks ago I killed one of those big boa-constrictor snakes. It was killing my chickens, so I watched for it and killed it. When I saw how beautiful it was, I decided to skin it and sell the skin. I had been told the skins are worth a lot of money. Well, as I was cleaning it," here he hesitated, and moved his body from side to side, then in a whisper he continued, "I accidentally stepped in some of its blood." He shuddered, then added, "I didn't have shoes on, and I had been told that the boa was a voo-doo snake and if I stepped in its blood I would die a very bad death. My family brought me here, but I told them you wouldn't know anything about witch doctoring. Why don't you just tell them to take me home?"

Jim gently placed his hand on the man's shoulder. "Senor," he began in a very quiet voice, "my God is greater than that voo-doo god. My God loves you and is not looking for ways to frighten you or get vengeance. I believe He can help you, if you will let me treat you."

The man agreed immediately and Jim treated him for anxiety. After a good nights sleep, he felt much better. His recovery was rapid, and he soon left the hospital. We heard that he went back to his village and told everyone that the Doctor in that hospital had a God greater than all gods they had heard about and he was going to learn more about Him.

"The Doctor said to tell you there is a patient who wants to meet you," one of the nurses called to me from the back porch. "He wants you to go over if you can." More and more this type of interruption of school was occurring, and more and more I had to pray for patience. Sometimes I felt that I never was allowed to finish one thing before there was something else that urgently needed my attention. I knew Jim would not call me during school hours unless it were truly important, so I left Billy to study by himself and went over to the hospital.

At first all I could see was her deformed face, then I noticed her twisted smile and sparkling eyes. "I asked the Doctor to call you," she said, holding my hand tightly in hers. "I promised my daughters I would meet the Doctor's wife and tell them how you look." She and two of her daughters were leper patients from down on the coast. She had come to sell dried fish and to take more medicine back home. "We want to know you, for we love the Doctor. We would be dead now if he had not gone to our village two years ago. Now we are almost well. Thank you and may God repay you."

I walked slowly back to the house. "Thank you, Lord," I whispered. "I am so very fortunate. Forgive my impatience and help me always to remember that You love these people, and died for them also."

Christmas without the Woods, especially their boys, who always livened up any meeting, was different but still did not lack for enthusiasm. We filled the usual bags of candy and practiced the pageant. The Christmas eve program was given before a yard packed with people. Many came from the villages around Ometepec and spent the night so they could attend the Christmas morning service of rejoicing and singing.

Soon the New Year started and we were told we would have a great shortage of water. From October until May, it seldom rains and wells refuse to produce clear water. Jim would have several large drums tied on to the truck to bring back water. Then they would pile on the dirty hospital laundry, and two women to wash clothes, and two men to fill the drums with water. He would take them about two miles to the small river where he would leave the women all day to wash the laundry. The drums would be filled with water and hauled back to the hospital.

In the afternoon, the children would ride out to the river to have their baths and play until the laundry was removed from the bushes. The sun had not only dried the laundered items but had also taken out most of the color. I dreaded these months with little or no water, but the children thought it was a wonderful time. I looked forward to the first rains, but they would always remind me that it was more fun to go to the river than to take baths.

I was always very careful to make everyone go up stream from the regular crossing of the animals and people who traveled from one town to another. I didn't know how far up stream from our swimming hole the next crossing was, but I hoped it was far enough for the water to become partially cleaned by the sand, rocks and sun.

One morning, before breakfast, I was called to the back porch by three of Dona Antonia's daughters. They often brought fresh fruits and vegetables from a cousin's farm, and this time the oldest girl handed me a beautiful melon. Then she surprised me with, "Senora, Chica is here." At first I couldn't remember who Chica was. Then from behind the three girls stepped a small girl in a dirty, ragged dress.

"Chica, you know, Lupe's sister." The girls laughed because I didn't recognize the girl. I was truly surprised and exclaimed, "Why, Chica, where did you come from? Your sister tried several times to find you after we heard your father had been killed." I recognized those large, sad eyes, and realized that life had never been easy for this child.

Her story was short and to the point. "I came from Cacahuatepec on the early plane. I was up in the mountains with my step mother and decided I wanted to find my sister. I remembered the verse she taught me, and I had heard that day that a woman in Cacahuatepec had Bible lessons in her house. So I got up before anyone was awake, and ran for a long time. Then I walked all the way to Cacahuatepec and looked up the woman I had heard them talking about. When she came to the door, I recited the verse, then asked her to help me find my sister. She asked me some questions, then put me on the plane and told me to find Don

Ramon, the dentist, when I got to Ometepec. Then Don Ramon told me you knew where my sister was and would help me. He said I couldn't go where she is. Is that true?"

It was a long speech for the child and she was completely out of breath when she finished. "Yes, it's true," I replied, "She is in Chihuahua in Nursing School. But we will write her today and tell her you are here. You can stay here until we can hear from her."

I didn't know what we would do with her. We would be leaving on furlough in a few weeks. Surely God had some plan He had not revealed to us yet. After she had bathed and put on clean clothes she looked much better and we had a long talk.

The next day Dona Antonia came to see me. She was smiling and said she knew I was wondering what to do with Chica while we were in the States. "Now, don't think anymore about it. Chica can stay with us and go to school with my girls. I have seven girls, and one more won't make any difference. If you can make her some clothes, we can certainly share our tortillas."

We hired Chica to help wash dishes in the hospital in the afternoon. She was a good worker, quiet but happy to be in a different living condition. She was a good student also, and was quick to learn. With her own money she bought her school supplies and felt proud to be able to help pay her own way.

The Woods returned from furlough in 1962 and we were to begin our furlough that summer. We had been looking for several months for a Mexican doctor to join us in Ometepec and to be director of the hospital while we were on furlough. Many were asked, but none wanted to live in southwest Mexico. Through the National Presbyterian Women's Society we heard about Alfredo Yanez, and Jim wrote to him. His mother was a Bible teacher and nationally know leader of women.

Again God had answered our prayers in a wonderful way. Dr. Yanez, with his wife and infant son joined our staff in 1962. We knew there was enough work for more than two doctors, but were thankful to have one to keep the hospital open while we were away. Much of the responsibility of running the hospital fell on Paula.

Our address from June 1962-63 was Tallahassee, Florida. We rented a house near Florida State University so our children could continue in the same schools. Jimmy was a junior at Florida State University, Peggi a junior in high school, Elizabeth in eighth grade and Billy in fifth grade in elementary school. Florence was the only one not at home. She had decided to go to her father's alma mater, Erskine College in South Carolina. Jim and I both were busy with speaking engagements both for church services and week-day women's meetings.

The year passed too fast and soon we were once more in the "throws" of packing. Jim had found many things he wanted to take back for the hospital and our stacks of boxes increased every day.

On our way back we were to stop in Dallas, Texas to speak at the Oak Cliff Presbyterian Church. As the plane landed I noticed a camera crew waiting at the foot of the steps. I turned to Billy and said, "Look, Billy, there must be someone of interest on this plane. Let's hurry off so we can see who it is." In our hurry we were separated from Jim by several people, but we rushed to the foot of the ramp and turned just in time to hear: "There he is. Hey, Doctor Boyce, look over here!" I saw the look of utter surprise on Jim's face change to a big grin as he saw our friend Dorothy Scoggins waving at him. At her feet was a wheelbarrow full of Green Stamp books. That night on television we saw it all over again, along with a report of the "Green Stamp Plane." Dorothy had not

Mr. and Mrs. Christie and Jim with "Messenger II," the Green Stamp plane. The Christies flew the plane into Ometepec on January 11, 1964.

only had a big part in getting the truck "Dorotea" and the saw mill, she had now opened her home as the Texas branch of the airplane project.

When Dorothy first heard about the Green Stamp plane she immediately wrote to the Christies in Florida and offered to help. With her customary enthusiasm and charm she rallied the women in the churches in Dallas to donate their precious books of stamps.

Again we realized how many people it takes to spread the love of our God around the world. Without people like the Eugene Boyces to take loving care of our children, and people like the Scoggins, and Christies and others in all the churches who had supplied the tools we needed to work, we could have done very little.

The day we arrived in Ometepec the children from Xochistlahuaca also arrived. There was much to be done in getting them ready for school, so there was no time for feeling sorry for ourselves in having to leave our children. All children in the Government schools wear uniforms. They are all made alike but each school has a different color. The treadle sewing machine was placed on the back porch so anyone who had time could sew. Yards of blue and white checked material were made into pinafores for the girls and shirts for the boys.

Soon after our hospital had opened, the government built a new elementary school across the street, so the children in that school did not have far to go. Those in high school, however, had to walk over a mile up town to their school. Their first class was at seven o'clock, then at nine o'clock, they had an hour to go home to eat breakfast. There was no lunch room at the school, so three times a day, the children in high school walked up town and back. Never once did they complain. Instead, they expressed over and over their gratitude in having a chance to study.

While on their furlough in 1961-62, the Woods had arranged for a young college graduate to come to Ometepec to teach their children. This would give Madge more time to prepare the material Johnny needed. This teacher stayed until the summer of 1963 and another came about the same time we returned from furlough. The new teacher, Christine, was from Florida. She had heard about the Green Stamp plane and was anxious to know when it would arrive.

The Christies had to wait until all stamps had been collected and acknowledged. Then negotiations with the company selling the type plane wanted had taken time. Finally, the place to deliver the plane to Mr. Christie was agreed upon and plans were now set for January 1964.

Paula West was leaving for furlough in the fall after our return and I knew I would have to spend more time in the hospital. Fortunately Billy was a good student and I could spend two or three hours in the morning with him, and he would work by himself until noon. We could work in odd times and neither of us minded.

The Christies finally reached Ometepec on January 11, 1964. They had a good flight down and declared the "Messenger II" a great little plane. Their visit was short but we enjoyed showing them the hospital, and Jim took Mr. Christie up for an aerial view of the region. They gave us a scrap book of letters and comments from churches all over the south about collecting the stamps. Most were humorous and enthusiastic. A few objecting. We were told that the only reason the Christies were given permission by the Board to collect stamps was that the Board was sure they could not separate that many stamps from the women.

Saviour, Thy dying love, Thou gavest me,
Nor should I aught with-hold; Dear Lord, from Thee:
In love my soul would bow, My heart ful-fill its vow.
Some offering bring Thee now, Something for Thee.

S.D. Phelps, D.D. 1899

Chapter XII

"The Last Full Measure"

Jim had several trips to outposts planned for the next few weeks, and Johnny had to go to Cuernavaca for the meeting of the General Assembly of the National Presbyterian Church of Mexico. Christine, the Wood children's teacher and Hilda, the Mexican mission worker, were to stay with the children. Johnny and Madge were to stop in Chilpancingo, then fly on to Mexico City. He needed to leave his plane in the City for a check-up while they were in Cuernavaca at the meeting.

Friday the seventeenth of January started like any Friday. Jim had surgery early, I was in the hospital for a short while, then started school with Billy. The plane from Acapulco flew overhead and landed at the airport.

Shortly after the plane landed, Luis, the agent for the airline, came dashing into the hospital. "Doctor Boyce," he called, "I've got to see the doctor," he told the nurse as he rushed past her. He met Dr. Yanez first and exclaimed, "Do you know where Johnny Wood is? There has been an airplane crash and the authorities in Mexico called Acapulco to ask about the Cessna plane XB-Jil." Jim had just come out of the operating room, but he rushed downtown without changing clothes to see if the telegraph office could give him any details. He could find no official news, just what people coming from Acapulco had heard.

He hurried back home to change clothes and called me into the bedroom to tell me what had happened. He would go to Acapulco, then on to Mexico City if he needed to go. He realized he was in too much of a state of shock to pilot the new plane himself. Also, he didn't think he should fly into Mexico City airport at midday.

"You will have to go tell Christine," he said to me. "Don't let the boys hear the news from people in the street. Bring them over here, and keep them inside until we find out if it's true or not."

In Acapulco he tried to call someone in the mission office but could not make connections, so he took the next flight to Mexico City. Edson Johnson, the mission business manager had been trying to send telegrams to us in Ometepec, but nothing had been confirmed at this point. The accident was in the mountainous region east of Cuernavaca and Jim, Edson, and another member of the Mission, Clarence Bassett, went to the little town of Chalco, about an hour's drive from Mexico City. In the municipal they were shown Johnny's log-book, a few papers belonging to John and Madge, their shoes, some clothing, and about a half of a Bible. The pages of the Book were whole, but the Bible had been ripped in two and only half was found. The men went back to Mexico City where Jim and Mr. Bassett were asked to identify the bodies. Jim said it was the hardest thing he ever had to do.

In the meantime, in Ometepec, I went to the Wood's house to tell Christine. I met Hilda in the yard and asked her to go tell Christine to leave the children with work to do and come meet me in the yard. Hilda saw I was very upset and immediately asked what had happened. "Go get Christine, then I'll tell you. But hurry," I said. I was afraid I would start crying and not be able to talk.

People were beginning to come by in droves, asking if it were true, and we did not want the children to hear about it from people in the street. Christine went back and finished the assigned school work then brought the boys over to our house. We told the children only that there had been an accident and that we were waiting for official word from Mexico. It was four thirty when that telegram arrived and the hard job of telling the children was given to me.

People began to come from all over the region to ask where the funeral was to be. I knew not where nor when. The day was long, but the night was longer. Van and Timmy came to me and asked if their parents could be buried next to Captain Brenton.

"I don't know, boys," I replied, "We will have to hear from your aunts in California before we can make plans. Uncle Jim and Kenton will probably come tomorrow and we can discuss plans."

I heard four year old Benji ask his brothers again, "Where is Mommy?" and the boys replied, "She has gone to see Jesus." Naturally Benji did not understand everything, but he knew something sad had happened, and he went from one person to another trying to cheer us up. The boys had received good Christian training in their short lives and we discussed life after death.

"We don't know why this happened," I answered many times that day. "We only know that Madge and Johnny have been taken from us. They are there, we are here and God wants us to keep living here until He calls us to join them."

That night after everyone was in bed Billy came and climbed in my bed. "I hope Daddy gets home all right tomorrow," he whispered. I knew his worry and once more assured him that God takes care of us, even when bad things happen.

In spite of trying to teach faith to everyone else, that night I lay awake asking God to give me more faith and wisdom in dealing with the next day. "What are we supposed to do? Who will carry on the work they have started? What will happen to these dear boys? Oh, dear Lord, I need some answers."

Early the next day a small plane flew in from Oaxaca. Mr. and Mrs. Bishop were the first to arrive. How relieved I was to see them! Floyd had lived here for the year the Woods were on furlough and knew the people in town. "How did you hear about the accident?" I asked.

"I heard it on the radio yesterday afternoon and called Mexico City to verify it. I believe Doctor Jim and Kenton will come via Acapulco today. I talked to Edson and he said he thought the funeral would be here. They are arranging a special flight from Mexico City on Monday. The relatives from California and friends from the National Church and Mission will be on it."

Jim did arrive Saturday afternoon. He had flown to Acapulco on the regular air line, then found one of the taxi planes from Ometepec about to return, so came on it. He said Kenton had stayed in Mexico City to meet the relatives from California on Sunday. They would all come on the charter plane on Monday.

They had all talked by telephone with the family in the States and they decided it best to have the funeral in Ometepec. I told Jim about the boys wish to have their parents buried next to Captain Brenton and he said he would have to ask the City Council.

Most cemeteries in small cities in Mexico are owned and operated by the City Council, and there are several ways to arrange burial. Jim would see the town President on Sunday.

As soon as Jim told the town President that the Woods were to be buried in Ometepec, he called a special meeting of the council. They looked at the map of the cemetery and decided that there was a plot just large enough for two coffins, if they were buried in crypt style. That would mean finding a brick mason who would work Sunday afternoon digging the grave and lining it with bricks, then building the above ground part early Monday. Jim said he had already had two men offer to do the work. (The first to offer had met Jim at the airport to tell him he would build the crypt if that was the type chosen for the grave. This man had worked on both houses and was an officer in the congregation.)

The City Council then did a very unusual and gracious thing. They deeded the cemetery lot to the heirs of John and Madge Wood as a gift from the City of Ometepec. It was their way of saying they appreciated what Johnny and Madge had done for the region.

The special plane arrived early from Mexico City and Kenton was the first one off. I was relieved when I saw him smile and greet his brothers. He had grown overnight from a high school student to man with responsibilities. We were all impressed with his clear thinking and his strong faith.

The coffins were removed from the plane and taken to the Woods front yard. There they were placed underneath the old tropical shade tree where Captain Brenton had prayed for the people of Ometepec. There the funeral service would be held for we knew the little church building would not begin to hold the crowd.

Nacho had come on the plane and he took charge of planning the funeral with the visiting ministers. There was much to be done but we truly felt upheld in the Christian love manifested by everyone.

On Tuesday just before the service, one of the women of the church asked me how we were planning to take the coffins from the house to the cemetery. It was well over a mile and we had planned to take them in the jeep truck but she shook her head. "Senora," she said, " you know it is customary here for the friends of the family to carry the coffins to the cemetery on their shoulders. The men have gathered and are planning how they will take turns carrying these two side by side, and I think you should talk to the family about it."

I went first to Jim, then we called the sisters in and explained the custom to them. "It is a beautiful tribute to Johnny and Madge," they said and agreed immediately.

Ometepec had never had a funeral like this one. Hundreds of people from the coastal plains and Indians from the mountains filled main street as the coffins were carried slowly through town and out to the cemetery. The local pilots flew over the procession and tipped their wings in salute.

"Be still my soul: thy God doth undertake
To guide the future as He has the past,
Thy hope, thy confidence, let nothing shake,
All now mysterious, shall be bright at last.
Be still my soul, the waves and wind still know
His voice who ruled them while He dwelt below."

From Psalm 46
Katharina vonSchlegel, 1752
translated by Jane Laurie Borthwick, 1855

Chapter XIII

Reorganizing and Looking Ahead

The afternoon after the funeral the sisters of Johnny and Madge met with Kenton to discuss what should be done about legal matters and personal possessions. I stayed away from all this as much as I could.

There was work to be done in the hospital, and somehow all these people from Mexico City and the States had to be fed. I was told that Dona Antonia, Mrs. Yanez and Mrs. Bishop were taking care of meals, so I went to help in the Drug Store.

It was here Johnny's sister found me and wanted to talk about the boys. She and her family were missionaries in Columbia, South America and just happened to be in California on furlough this month. She understood more than Madge's sisters about living in another country. Van Wood had told her that he and his brothers did not want to leave Ometepec. This was their home and they had many friends they did not want to leave. She wondered if we thought we would be able to keep them.

"You know we love those boys," I said, "and you know we would keep them if it were possible and feasible. However, there are many things to be considered. Madge's youngest sister is named their guardian and she wants the boys to go to a good school. I think they should be kept together as long as they are small, if at all possible." I hesitated then added an idea Jim and I had discussed the night before. "Why not leave the four boys in Ometepec until next summer. That is, if Christine is willing to stay. They can finish the school year and the family in the states can straighten out legal matters without being in a hurry.

"We feel very strongly that it would be best for the boys to leave them here for awhile. They have lost both mother and father very suddenly. If they should now lose home, friends and their pet animals just as suddenly, it would have a much greater psychological effect on them.

"They have grown up in Ometepec, in fact Jim delivered Benji in this hospital. They call us Aunt and Uncle and have been in our house almost as much as their own. Now, if the family agrees, the boys can move in with us and Christine can have Paula's room. Hilda can move in with the nurses. The family will have time to make plans and prepare for the move. We can move all of Johnny and Madge's personal belongings into the basement of the hospital where they will be safe until arrangements can be made to ship them."

"Thank you," the aunt said, "I shall suggest this to Kenton. If he thinks it all right we shall talk it over with the others."

The cause of the crash had been on everyone's mind and the Mexican Government had inspectors on the site as soon as they could reach the isolated region. The only eye-witness had been a farmer who said he was working in his field when he heard a loud "boom". He looked up and saw a plane come through the clouds and a wing fly off. The plane broke into parts and spread over a large area. There was no sign of fire.

When the Woods had left Cuernavaca that noon to drive back to Mexico City, several of the women gathered to bid Madge good-by. They said that Madge looked up to the cloudy, windy sky and remarked, "I don't like to fly in this kind of weather, but Johnny needs to be back tonight for prayer meeting." That was the last any of them remember her saying.

Our good friend Senor Barcenas, the airplane mechanic in Chilpancingo, heard about the crash early Friday and immediately had flown to Mexico City. He went to the Cessna repair shop to talk to the mechanics who had worked on the plane. The two men who had done the work were not there that day, but the other men on duty told Senor Barcenas that when Johnny left the plane they had told him they were too busy to take it for three or four days. Johnny had then told some of the mechanics he would be willing to pay "off-duty" prices to have it repaired while he was in Cuernavaca because it was urgent that he return to Ometepec on Wednesday.

Johnny had returned in mid-afternoon, paid his bill, and even though the weather was "marginal" he decided to go ahead. The official inspector of planes had not seen the plane as the work was done as "off-duty" work and not official Cessna repair.

Senor Barcenas left Mexico City and came straight to Ometepec for the funeral and to report what he had learned in Mexico City. Later he returned to Mexico City, and did several days of intensive investigation as to the cause of the crash. He reported to us that no conclusive reason for the crash had been given.

Kenton was due back in school and all three aunts had families back home. Time was set to return to the States. Finally, the aunts called Jim and me in and thanked us for our help the past week. They agreed to leave the four youngest boys with us until July. Then the guardian and her family would come down for a month's vacation and take the boys back with them.

After the plane with the last of the visitors left Ometepec we rushed home to move furniture. Our dining room was turned into a dormitory. We had long before started eating our meals on the back porch where it was cooler. We had set up beds several times in the dining room when we had visitors.

The boys brought with them a beautiful cocker spaniel, a loud parrot, and a pet rabbit someone had given Benji. Billy's large German shepherd and the Spaniel had been friends since Christmas. The parrot was a friend to no one and evidently did not like his new location, for he squawked every time anyone entered the room. The rabbit was in a screened wooden box and was supposed to stay in it. However he was much faster than his little master and soon escaped.

Jim and Benji both were early risers and each morning just at daylight Jim would take Benji on his shoulders for a walk to listen to all the birds. Often Benji looked for nests during the day and would guide Jim to his new find the next morning.

In the afternoons Van, Timmy, Danny, and Billy liked to ride their very old and much worn bicycles on some designated trail. They were good about telling me where they intended to go but often would see something else to tempt them. I very seldom worried for they usually showed up before our meal time.

Once after a rather long ride they came in tired and very upset. "What in the world is the matter?" I asked as they threw down their bikes and stomped into the house.

All four answered, "The road is coming into town. They have reached Las Vigas and will be in town by next week."

"Well, why should that upset you?" I asked.

"That road will ruin everything," Van declared.

"Yeah, we won't be able to ride our bikes for all the cars!" Billy added.

"They drove the donkeys off this afternoon, " Timmy said. "And that's the way they have always come into town. We wish the road would never come into Ometepec."

I was surprised the boys were so concerned and told them the road was progress for the region and people would be able to have a bus ride to other towns, even Mexico City.

"They don't need that," Van insisted, "That road will just ruin this town for children. Before long the road will be full of trucks and cars and children won't be allowed to ride bikes on it."

"And they will make all the animals get off,too."

"And that's just not fair! The animals were here first!"

I was puzzled about the boys not wanting the road because everyone else in town had been wanting that road for years. I finally came to the conclusion that it was because these boys loved their freedom in Ometepec and were deeply concerned about any change. Then I started pointing out all the new and wonderful changes a connection to the outside world would bring.

Electricity had been added to the city several years back, but only from six to twelve at night. Recently the poles to bring electricity from a large new hydroelectric dam near the capitol of the state had been brought along the new road. We could soon have electricity twenty-four hours a day.

"You boys don't remember when we couldn't even buy a light bulb in Ometepec, do you?"

"Electricity is O.K., but not the road." one of them said, and I decided that nothing would change their minds at this time, so told them to bathe for supper.

In all the events of the past months we had almost forgotten about the new carry-all that had been ordered with the extra Green Stamp books. When we received the notice that it was ready and we could pick it up everyone was excited. Mission meeting was to be at the YMCA camp near Cuernavaca very soon. We needed a vehicle larger than the jeep to carry this family.

We needed to buy shoes for all the boys, also, and Ometepec still did not have a large selection of regular shoes. Cuernavaca is over six thousand feet above sea level, so the climate is quite a contrast to our tropical climate.

When I walked into the nice shoe store in Mexico City with the five boys and one of the girls living with us, the clerk looked down the row of children and asked, "Are these all of the same family?" Before I could say anything one of the children replied, "Oh, no, there are five in the States in school."

How nice, I thought, to be considered by the children as one big family made me very happy, and I did not explain anything to the clerk. He looked at me in awe, and I just smiled and said that all of them needed shoes.

At Mission meeting, it was voted that the Bassetts would move to Ometepec the summer of 1964. They, too, had a large family. They were planning to move in June or July. Madge's sister with her husband and three children were coming in July for a month. Kenton would come as soon as school let out in June. It was to be a busy time, indeed.

Christine finished the year's school work with the boys in June and I truly hated to see her leave. She had been a wonderful teacher and friend to the boys during these months. Billy finished his school year also and I was glad not to have that responsibility during the summer. Paula returned and took up her work in the hospital. She now had a degree in anesthesiology and the hospital operating room was updated.

To say the six months had been easy and all rosy, would not be entirely true. Like any family there had been days of sibling rivalry and disagreements. However, it had been a very easy time, considering the trauma we had all been through. Van again vowed to run away rather than go to California. I was glad Kenton was there to talk to him. I wanted him to know we loved him and would keep all of them if we could, yet I had to make him understand he would have to go.

On the day the boys were to leave with their new family, many young people gathered to see them off. Most of the church members had also come. There were tears and many memories recalled as I looked at the boys and thought of their parents. I hugged them good-by and stepped back to watch the door of the plane close.

"That chapter of our lives has closed," I thought. "Lord give us grace and guidance as we start a new chapter."

Kenton had not left with the other boys. He was left in Ometepec to finish taking care of the few material possessions and delivering some gifts to some of their friends. Their beautiful Cocker Spaniel had been left and Kenton wanted to investigate ways to take the dog to the States. Van and Timmy had been very upset when told they could not take their dog. It had been a Christmas present from Madge and Johnny their last Christmas.

It took several trips to Acapulco, trips to the vet and many papers to fill out, but when Kenton was ready to join his brothers in California, the dog was also ready.

One of the patients in the hospital was a Bible teacher from near Acapulco. He had a giant cell tumor in one leg.

Jim had him come to the hospital when some surgeons from Tallahassee, Florida were there. Doctors Hank Watt and Jim Conn removed the tumor and told him he must not walk on the leg for several weeks. The patient not only taught Bible, but was an excellent teacher of reading and writing. So while he was in the hospital he would have classes around his bed.

On another bed in the same room was a man from Benito Juarez, a new ranch down on the coastal plains. He wanted to learn to read, and before he left the hospital he had a good start. A few weeks after he left, Jim and Don Ramon received an invitation to attend the official inaugural celebration of Benito Juarez. Jim had treated many patients from that ranch and Don Ramon thought we ought to go.

We left at six o'clock the morning of March 21, a national holiday honoring Benito Juarez, a statesman and President of Mexico from 1868-1872. Paula had arranged to get the day off. Billy invited Bobby, Don Ramon and his wife Dona Lupe. Jim and I were all excited about seeing part of the country we had never seen. We took breakfast and supper but knew we would have barbecue with the ranchers at noon.

The road was paved the first part of the trip and there were three new bridges. However, when we reached Rio Verde, about fifty miles from our destination, we crossed the river on an old time barge. The road from there on was about six inches deep with dark, fine dust. (The people told us later that in the rainy season this becomes such deep mud that not even tractors can get through.)

About ten o'clock we saw the improvised shade where the fiesta was to be held. The red,white and green flag of Mexico was waving briskly in the breeze coming from the Pacific Ocean just a few miles away.

One house had been turned into a clinic for the Doctor and nurse to see patients for two hours. Town officials came for all of us at twelve o'clock to escort us to the celebration.

There were children everywhere. Most of the colonists of the new town were young families. Most of the young women were pregnant or carrying a baby in her rebozo, or both. They were healthier than most children we had seen along the way. Most wore shoes or sandals. All were clean and dressed for the big celebration of naming the town.

We had known that Jim and Don Ramon were special guests of honor, but we were not prepared, nor ever dreamed, that Jim would be asked to say a few words, lead in prayer, and actually unveil the portrait of Benito Juarez.

We were also told that in the center of town was a lot for a Presbyterian Church. Several of the men told Jim that afternoon that they knew very little about our religion, but what they knew was what they wanted their children to learn. They borrowed Jim's Bible and passed it around reading portions. We gave out Bible portions and sold some Bibles, and promised to send more. It was a very happy, interesting holiday and we looked forward to returning sometime in the future. It was late when we reached Ometepec that night, and fortunately there was no emergency that night.

The day after a holiday was always a busy one in the hospital. Their fiestas usually had alcohol drinks of all kinds and quite often the day ended with fights. Men always carried machetes with them for legitimate reasons: killing snakes, clearing paths of fallen branches, etc. Also it made a man feel "macho." Unfortunately, when drunk this feeling sometimes made him use his machete on human beings.

On the day after our outing to Benito Juarez, Jim was called to see a woman with a cut across her head and one on her arm. They sewed her scalp and arm and when she was back in her room Jim asked her mother what had caused the fight.

"That man asked her for a dance and she said no. He asked her a second time and she said no again, so he pulled out his machete and hit her on the head, then the arm. He was drunk, and that was why she didn't want to dance with him."

Now that the road made it easier to come to the hospital, Jim was called more and more for accident cases, machete cuts, and gun shot wounds. As more trucks were bought by the business men to haul merchandise from Acapulco, and automobiles bought by families who traveled by planes before, the airlines began to lose passengers. The road to town that ran just a few yards from the hospital became very busy and I often remembered the day our boys had proclaimed that the road would ruin the street for boys on bicycles.

Jim was asked by some of the business men in town to be a charter member of a Lions Club. He was pleased they had asked him. They did not have a place to meet, so they met in homes of the members. It was a wonderful chance for him to get to know the men on more of a social and business basis.

Several times since the opening of the hospital, doctors from the states had visited Ometepec in work teams. Eyes had been examined for the first time. Surgeons came to do difficult cases. Dr. Roger Hehn, Jacksonville, Florida, a specialist in facial surgery, brought a team of doctors to repair hare-lips. Jim asked the Lion's Club to sponsor announcements over the radio about the project. The doctors would charge nothing and the hospital only what the patient could pay.

We had not realized how far and wide those little plastic radios could carry a message. The Acapulco Lions Club joined in the project, so towns on the northern end of the coast of Guerrero also heard the news. The day before the doctors arrived, patients from miles away had gathered. Small babies, half-grown children, and adults lined up.

When the doctors stepped into the room where they were waiting, one doctor was almost overcome with the sight. "That's more hare-lips than I saw during all my years of medical training!" he exclaimed.

The doctors worked from early morning until late at night, and still there were patients waiting. Most of them had never thought anything could be done for their unnatural looks. Many blamed their disfigurement on "the clees." Few had ever thought it could be a hereditary condition.

The doctors were there for the week before Easter and some patients did not arrive until Thursday. When told they were too late, many said they would wait in town to see if there just might be a cancelation of someone already on the list for surgery. When Dr. Hehn promised to return the next year at the same time, some patients wanted to sign up a year in advance.

The gratitude of those who did receive surgery was touching. One Indian man whose child had been one of the first to have surgery, walked all day to go home and bring back a goat as a present. It was a large goat and we had it barbecued for the last meal the doctors were there.

Dr. Hehn has returned with a team of doctors each Easter week for over twenty years. Word of their work has spread high up into the mountains and up the Pacific coast of the state of Guerrero. Hundreds of operations have given new life to many patients who had always covered their faces when near another person.

Bode, one of the taxi pilots, was a member of the Lions Club. He was known for his rough language and sense of humor. He was always very nice to us and was especially kind and thoughtful at the time of the Wood crash. He knew the region of southwest Guerrero like the palm of his hand and could land on the trickiest air-strips.

It was a shock to everyone, then, when Bode had a crash and was killed on the Ometepec air field. He had worked on his plane with two other mechanics that day, and in the afternoon took it up for a test flight. Something happened and the motor stopped and Bode tried to glide down to the field. The Ometepec air-strip had a steep bluff at the end of approach and Bode's plane missed the airstrip by just a few yards.

After the funeral, the Lions Club called a special meeting to honor Bode and do something for his family. At this meeting some of the men asked the question: "Is there life after death?" They all turned to Jim for the answer. He took out his pocket testament and read several passages about the hereafter and what happens after death. They had some profound questions that needed answers from a higher authority than any of them, so Jim quoted scriptures and catechism. "We are not to judge who goes to heaven and who does not," he told them. "God is the judge, not man. Only God knows a man's inner heart." There followed a long discussion and when they finally dismissed the meeting the men thanked Jim for the comfort and advice he had given.

> "O Master from the mountain side
> Make haste to heal these hearts of pain
> Among these restless throngs abide
> O tread the city's streets again."

Where Cross the Crowded Ways of Life, ver.5
Frank Mason North, 1903

Chapter XIV

Floods and Beans

The year 1965 found many changes in the personnel of our mission staff in Ometepec. After a term in Ometepec, The Bassetts had been moved to Campeche. Edna Garza, a registered nurse from Texas, had been sent to help Paula with the growing amount of work in the hospital. Dr. Yanez was still with us and another doctor had been given privilege to bring patients and help with surgery. I was given more on the job instructions in daily book keeping. I opened an office in our house where I could work with fewer interruptions.

The summer of 1965 was filled to overflowing with church activities, summer visitors, and hospital work. Florence finished college and came home for the summer. Peggi and Elizabeth joined her. Jimmy was the only one who could not come. He was in graduate school at Florida State, had a job working in the physics department, and was also taking a course or two to make his fall load easier.

Edna's brother, Dan, a second year student at Austin Presbyterian Seminary, and two young women were sent by the Board to be summer workers for the church. Dan was an accomplished musician and knew Spanish, so was immediately named the summer pastor. Florence brought her violin, and we had more music than at any time since the days the Woods were with us. There were piano duets, piano-violin duets, singing in all kinds of groups, and music in the services that lifted our souls and minds and brought back the joy our lives had missed for some time.

We had welcome parties, good-by parties, birthday parties, and just parties. Our summer workers had Bible schools, day schools and Sunday schools. The summer workers visited the

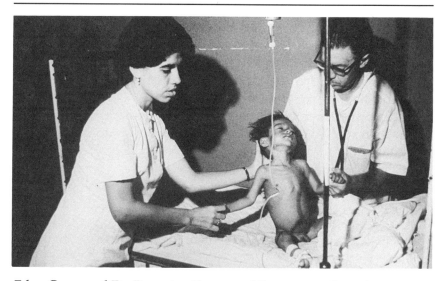

Edna Garza and Dr. Boyce treating one of the many patients for dehydration.

congregations in as many small towns as they could manage in the time they were there. At night our house was the center of activities for playing games, practicing special pieces of music, or listening to those who practiced. The summer passed entirely too fast and our lives divided to go separate ways. However, we had stored up many happy memories to pull up later when we needed them.

In 1966, Billy finished elementary school at home and took tests to enter preparatory school in the U.S. He did very well on his SSAT exam and was offered a scholarship at McCallie School in Chattanooga, Tennessee. (Eugene and Louise Boyce had gone to Ethiopia to serve under U.S. Aid, and our children had scattered.) Jimmy had received his Master's at Florida State and would move to Duke University to work on his Doctorate. Florence had taught a year at Florence, S.C., and announced her engagement to Dan Garza, the wedding to be in August. Dan still had one year to finish Seminary, but they had decided that two could easily live on what they would save on telephone bills. Peggi was a sophomore at Florida State. Elizabeth was a junior in high school and staying with friends in Atlanta, Georgia.

We took the month of August as our vacation and rushed up

to Texas. Florence wanted her father to perform the ceremony. As a foreigner, he could not marry people in Mexico, so they asked to have the service in Dan's home church in Harlingen, Texas. Dan's father had been an elder in this church for years, so he was pleased that Florence and Dan had chosen their church.

At most conventional weddings, the mother of the bride knows everyone. At this one, I only knew Dan's parents. The church was full for the ceremony and over two hundred people were at the reception.

Immediately after the wedding we climbed into our carry-all and headed for Florida. We let Peggi and Jimmy off at Florida State dorms and continued on to Atlanta. Elizabeth was already two days late for school and we should have been in Chattanooga two days before for Bill.

It was not easy to leave that last child. Some friends remarked that I had left children so often, I was surely going to take it as a natural thing to do. Not so. It was harder with each child and I prayed all the way back to Ometepec for God to give me grace and strength. "Lord," I prayed, "My heart is so downcast right now. I know Your grace is sufficient for us, so I am asking for a little extra at this time. Please, fill my void with satisfying jobs for you."

When we arrived in Ometepec, we found some new children from Xochistlahuaca to stay with us. Linda, who had been with us during the previous year, brought her younger sister, Bequi. Another sister was staying with Don Ramon and Dona Lupe. Bequi was shy, knew little Spanish, but had a good sense of humor. It didn't take long for her to be at the head of her first grade class.

I was called over to the hospital a day or two after we returned and was told that an Indian woman in the woman's ward wanted to talk to me. She didn't know very much Spanish, but it didn't take me long to know what she wanted. She had six boys and one girl, Josefina. The girl was ten or eleven years old and had been studying Amusgo with Amy in Xochistlahuaca. However, she had never been to school. "Please, Senora," the mother begged, gripping my hand tightly, "Let my daughter stay with you to go to school. Give her a chance to be somebody. She is smart. If she stays in the village she will not have a chance.

Please, Senora, give her a chance."

"But don't you need her to help you?" I asked.

"I will work harder. Please, she needs a chance."

I promised to talk it over with Doctor Boyce and the girls who were already crowded in their two rooms. Linda and Bequi seemed to know the mother was going to ask us to take Josefina, and immediately agreed to make room for her. "Bequi and I can sleep in one bed," Linda said, "we are used to sleeping with more than two to a bed."

When I asked Jim he said anything we arranged would be all right with him. The mother had come in to have her seventh child and had asked the doctor please to tie her tubes so she would have no more. She and her husband had learned to read in Amusgo and were leaders in the congregation in their village.

So Josefina joined our ever growing family and I soon found out she was not only very intelligent, she was full of energy and ambition. (She later became the first woman President of her village.)

That year the rains started early and were quite heavy. Then in September, just at the end of rainy season a tropical storm rolled into that region. Rain poured down from morning until night. Jim and I were listening to it pound on the roof when we heard the back door of the hospital slam shut. Then we saw the flash light coming toward our window. "Oh, dear," I lamented, "I bet you have to go deliver a baby in this storm."

"Babies love to come during storms and Sundays," Jim said as he quickly dressed. "This is both Sunday and stormy, so we'll probably have more than one tonight." He, of course, knew there were three women in the labor room.

Rain was pouring off the roof in a solid sheet as he started out. The driveway was a river carrying the water down to the street. Bright flashes of lightning split across the sky, followed quickly by menacing thunder rolling and echoing through the mountains. It rained all day Monday, all night and again all day and night on Tuesday. Wednesday we heard that San Juan was under water and the bridge washed out. The coastal plains were under water and many people and animals washed down the rivers.

Jim had been required to leave Messenger II at the border the month before. He needed some other paper to get a Mexican license, and until he was granted that permit he had to fly it to the border every six months for a renewal permit. Now he wished he had it, for we heard the road had been washed out by landslides between Ometepec and the village of San Juan.

The town President and a group of business men drove as far as they could, then borrowed horses to survey the damages. One of the taxi pilots, Beto, took off to make one of his regular trips. He returned with a tragic report. Jim was on his way to the airport when he met Beto returning. "Oh, Doctor," he said, shaking his head in disbelief, "There are people hanging to the tops of coconut trees. They waved at me, but I could find no place to land. It is awful, simply awful. The crops are gone, houses gone and I'm sure many people are lost."

The town President came back to report that there had been five land slides between Ometepec and San Juan. He immediately ordered crews of men to clear the road so trucks could get through.

All school children were sent home to ask for clothing and already prepared food. The Army was put in charge of distributing packages to isolated families and towns along the coast. They had already requested helicopters, but received word the 'copters were busy rescuing people north of Acapulco.

People were generous with their food, but worried about food holding out in Ometepec. Two truck loads of food were gathered, wrapped in water proof plastic bundles, and dropped where people had gathered on higher ground.

Just before noon a Cessna plane flew over the hospital and signaled to Jim to go to the airport. Milton Anderson, a Missionary Aviation Pilot, had heard over the radio of the flood on the coastal region of Guerrero, and had flown over from his station in Oaxaca to help out. He had seen the devastated land for miles as he approached Ometepec. He and Jim and the Army Colonel held a conference on what needed to be done.

Jim and Mr. Anderson took a load of medicines and food and flew to one of the villages that Jim knew would be above the flooded water. The town of about four hundred inhabitants was over flowing with nearly a thousand who had managed to reach the higher ground. Every house was opened to the victims of the floods and the two room school house had been divided with men in one room and women in the other.

Everyone seemed to rush at the plane when it stopped. "Oh, Doctor, we were hoping you would come," they greeted the two men. The town President came pushing through the crowd. "Doctor, I hope you brought something for fever. Many of these people already have fever. I just ordered the men to vacate their room at the school house so you can have a place to hold clinic. Our food is also out, and many have not eaten for two days."

Milton helped Jim set up to see the sick, then flew back to Ometepec to take food to other villages. He said he would return in time to take him back to Ometepec before dark.

Jim worked all day and his medicine was running low when Milton returned. The line of sick was still long, and Milton looked at his watch. "Keep working, Jim, you can have another half hour. I can't make another trip from Ometepec today, so I'll just wait for you."

A half hour later Milton came in and called Jim to look at the sky. The mountains toward Ometepec were covered with another dark rain cloud, and the two men decided they would not be able to get back that night. They would spend the night and leave

People arriving from flooded area to small town of Buenos Aires, a village built on higher ground than most ranches.

early the next morning. Jim kept on seeing patients until he ran out of medicine.

"How long were you in the water?" was his first question to each patient. Most of them answered "two days." When asked how they had arrived at this place, they said they had clung to a floating tree, or piece of house or anything flowing by. Women tied their babies on their backs, and small children clung tightly to the backs of older siblings or relatives. Many people had muck itch from walking in the mud for so long.

About dark someone brought in a lamp so the Doctor could see some more patients. He wrote down their names and what medication they needed. He promised to send the medication the next day.

The food they had brought that morning was not enough for more than one day. The leaders decided to feed everyone once that day and save the rest for children. It was the first food many had eaten in two days.

About two hours after sunset, Don Juan, the village president, came in with two cots for Jim and Milton. The doctor's instruments were packed up and he and Milton lay down to rest. The other men were allowed to find sleeping room on the floor. Only the two visitors had cots.

Early the next morning Jim heard two men talking. One groaned and said, "Ay, it's this awful hunger in my stomach that keeps me awake. This terrible anguish that won't go away. Are we going to all starve before we can get more to eat?"

As soon as it was daylight enough to take off, Jim and Milton started toward the plane. Suddenly they heard shouts for them to wait. One of the few cows left in the village had been milked and everyone wanted the two men to have a glass of milk before leaving. Neither of them wanted to take the milk. "Give it to the children," they both said, "We will be back in Ometepec in twenty minutes."

"Oh, no, Doctor," Don Juan said, "You did not eat last night and our hospitality would be amiss if you did not partake of something before you leave. Everyone wants you to have a glass of milk. It is all we have to offer you, so please drink, even just a small glass would make us feel better."

So Jim and Milton each drank a small glass of warm milk and

thanked the people for being so generous.

When they reached Ometepec, they received the news that the helicopters had not arrived and they had lost connections on the radio. Milton asked permission of the Colonel to fly to Acapulco with a written request for food and help. Two small planes were dispatched, Milton had the written order, the other was to bring back immediately what he could in food supplies.

Before they arrived in Acapulco, Milton saw why they had not been able to get the helicopters to Ometepec. The upper coast and Acapulco were flooded and the situation was indeed serious. As Milton landed, one of his tires went flat, and he had to taxi to a repair shop. It took him longer, but when he reached the General in charge of relief work, he heard good news. The United States was sending more helicopters and several cargo planes of food. They would send one helicopter that afternoon to Ometepec. They would have to examine the field in Ometepec to see if the cargo plane could land there.

Milton, remembering the moans of hunger of his room mates the night before, asked permission to take a load of food to Buenos Aires. He told the General about the crowd of people he had left hungry. "I will stop in Ometepec for the medicine Doctor Boyce will have ready for me, then take both food and medicine to Buenos Aires this afternoon."

The General was very agreeable and ordered a jeep to take food and help load up Milton's plane. "Tell them a 'copter will be there as soon as we can dispatch it," he instructed Milton.

When Milton reached Ometepec, Jim was waiting with the medicine for the people in Buenos Aires. Milton delivered the messages to the Colonel, and said he would return to Oaxaca after delivering this load to Buenos Aires.

That night Jim studied his map of the region and wrote down the names of the villages where he was sure they needed food. He made several copies and put them in his shirt pocket, so he would have them the next day.

Early Saturday morning we heard the whirling props of the helicopters and Jim rushed to the airport. When he arrived, he found the Commander of the American Operation and the Mexican Colonel were having communication problems. They both were glad to see an interpreter. The Commander immediately stepped off the length of the field and shook his head. "This is not long enough for the cargo plane to make a landing," he said to Jim. "Is there a longer field nearby that is not covered with water.?"

"Yes, about twenty-five Kilometers away is the town of Cuajinicuilapa. It is higher than most of the coast." Jim said.

"Can you take me there?" the Commander asked, and Jim turned to the Colonel and explained what the Commander wanted. The three men then boarded the 'copter and went to Cuajinicuilapa to examine the field there. Finding it satisfactory, they decided to make this the headquarters for the relief operation. Jim was brought back to Ometepec that afternoon. The Colonel remained to discuss plans with the town Council.

Sunday morning Beto took Jim to Cuajinicuilapa at day break. Soon eight helicopters appeared on the coastal horizon, followed by the largest cargo plane these people had ever imagined. They discussed where people would be stranded and Jim pulled out his list. The Colonel looked it over and asked if he might use it. The Commander asked if he could have a copy. Soon the 'copters began distributing food. The plan was to leave a ton of food in each place unless it was an organized town, where they could leave as much as three tons.

The third day the Governor of the State arrived and asked Jim to fly with him and name all the flooded villages. First, he wanted to find a town they had flown over on the way to Cuajinicuilapa. "The people were on a knoll used for a basket ball court, and down the middle of the court they had spelled out `alimentos' (food) with coconuts. They waved and shouted, but there was no place for a plane to land. Now if we can fly back I'd like to drop some food." They found the place, and after circling the field, they dropped the food right in middle of the basket ball court. The people jumped on the package like children after a pinata is broken.

Had it not been such a tragic time you could have said that Jim was having a time of his life. He was thrilled to be asked to help with the operation and especially enjoyed riding in the helicopters. By the end of the week, however, he was exhausted and exclaimed,"I have seen more hardship and suffering this week than ever before in my life."

The road to Acapulco was soon opened with barges crossing the rivers with trucks and dugout canoes carrying people. It would be months before the pavement was replaced.

One of the things needed immediately was clothes, especially pants for the men. I had sent a telegram about the flood to friends in Mexico City and they had collected clothes and sent them on the plane immediately. Unfortunately, most were for women and children and the men were in desperate condition. Then we received a check from a church in the States and Jim and the men in charge of the relief program asked if the money could be spent to buy men's blue jeans. I was asked to go make the purchase, and wired a friend to meet me and go with me.

We decided to go straight to the factory and boldly ask for a special price. The man in charge of the sales department was surprised that two American women were buying several hundred pairs of men's pants, and even more surprised that we were going to give them away to victims of the flood. Furthermore, he believed us, and gave us a very good price.

The English speaking Union Church in Mexico City had also collected clothing for me to take back, and I had to plead for the airline to take it as excess baggage. They saw the large boxes and wanted to send it the next week as cargo, but when I explained it was for the flood victims, and would be distributed that very afternoon, they put it on.

Paula and another missionary went to Buenos Aires and a neighboring village to give out clothes. Paula was amused that so many women would take dresses much too large, but were so glad to have something clean they didn't care. One woman remarked, "I will wear it like this until I can find a sewing machine, then I'll make two out of it." The men used the ropes we had tied around the boxes for belts. Smiles and tears of appreciation were all they had to pay with, and all that was needed.

Everyone worked hard the next few days. Some official sent a gasoline pump to install in a well in one of the towns. There followed a long discussion about how to get the pump to the village and if the people could make it run. Finally the Colonel gave the order for them to take it in one of the planes. He turned to Jim and after saying a few words to express his frustration, he said, "I could not make him understand that the village is still primitive.

You and I know there is no gasoline within miles of that place. But let them put it in. Then they can tell people back in Mexico City they installed a pump in a well so the people can have clean water. They won't have to tell anyone that they had no way to run the thing!"

The helicopters returned to Acapulco after distributing the food, but the diseases that follow in the path of a flood stayed with us for weeks.

On October 30, Jim had a bad fall and fractured his seventh dorsal vertebra. We had been kept awake all night by a kitten that had somehow climbed up onto our roof. The mother cat would call to it from the ground and the kitten answer from the roof. Jim finally, in desperation, decided he would get that kitten down. What he did not realize in the dark was that the roof was very slick with wet moss. His feet slipped from under him and he knew immediately as he hit that he had hurt his spine.

I had heard the thud, but thought it was the ladder, so did not get up. Jim lay still until he saw the night watchman circle the hospital. "Don Adolfo," he called, "go get some men to get me down."

It was still dark, and Don Adolfo did not know where Jim was. As Jim was not shouting, he did not shout in reply.

"Doctor, I hear you, but don't see you."

"I'm on the roof of my house and I have hurt my back. Get some men to help me down."

I am ashamed to admit it, but as soon as that cat quit crying, I immediately went sound asleep. I did not hear the men come, nor did I see them as they rolled Jim to the hospital on the stretcher. He directed the entire process, how the men could move him, and how the nurse was to take an x-ray. Then he instructed the men to wheel him back to the house.

By that time I was awake and informed about the early morning incident. Dr. Yanez was called, also Paula and all of us had a conference. Jim did not want to stay in the hospital. Period! A hospital bed could be put up in our living room, and from there he could do much of his paper work. We gave in finally, and I knew it would be easier for everyone, especially for me, to have him in the house.

The first three or four days were difficult, but soon we were having committee meetings, staff meetings, church meetings, visitors, etc. all around his bed in our living room.

One Sunday afternoon when Nacho was in Ometepec, he and a group of men representing the outpost congregations came to talk to Jim about a need in the entire region. The flood waters had receded, but the entire crop of corn, sesame, and vegetables in the costal region had been lost. The men in the villages said that if they had black beans to plant right now, they could get a crop before the ground became parched again.

The government had promised them beans to plant, and they were now in Acapulco. Trucks could not cross the Papagallo River yet, so if the farmers would go to Acapulco they would be given the beans. The farmers were indignant. How could they go to Acapulco? And even if they could go, how could they bring back so many beans? It would take two tons to replant enough for food just for the people to eat, with none to sell.

One of the church men from up in the mountains had come with news and a suggestion. The Indians up higher in the mountains had just harvested their beans and had a good yield. Now they had no way to get the beans out to the market. What about sending three men from the church to buy beans from the Indians and haul them to Buenos Aires so the farmers there could plant and have food in a very few weeks.

The big question was "How would we get the beans down the mountain?" It would take many donkeys and several days. Every day was crucial, as the growing time was short.

Then one of the Ometepec men remembered that a young man in town had bought a new truck just before the floods and needed to haul something in order to make his payment on the truck. What if they asked him if he could make this trip? His truck could carry two tons, but they would have to pay him. Did the church have enough money?

Nacho suggested that they go ask the man if he could go in his truck. "Maybe we need to step out in faith. We know the people are hungry and food will be hard to find for a long time. Maybe God is telling us to feed the people with our few loaves, and He will multiply them."

The next day we received a telegram from the States asking if we could use some more money in the flood relief. I sent one of the children up town to send a telegram in reply, and to tell Nacho we needed to talk.

Two days later the men from the church left to purchase the beans, and Nacho went to Buenos Aires with two of the officers in the congregation in Ometepec. Don Juan was elated when he heard what they were doing and called the men of the town together.

"Each man will say how much land he has that he can plant. He will be given the customary measurement of so many quarts of beans per acre. I will keep a record and we will know how much your beans have multiplied.

When the men returned they again gathered around Jim's bed and told of their project. "We know you are back here praying for us, for only God could have gotten us through some of those hard places. It was a four wheel drive truck and he had a winch, but, we'll tell you in truth, Doctor, that truck is now well initiated into running on rural roads."

Jim soon asked me to take his x-rays and measurements to a class-mate of his in Mexico City. This was a doctor of German background who had gone on to do graduate studies in Philadelphia and also in Germany. He was an excellent orthopedist. The Doctor was very nice and studied the x-ray carefully. "Jim was very fortunate, you know. A little more and he could have been very seriously injured. I'll order a brace immediately and tell them to have it ready for you to take back day after tomorrow. Then tell him I want to see him as soon as he can come to the City."

The beans grew fast in the soft ground, and we heard they had a very good yield. Then one day Don Juan came in with his satchel and asked to see Jim and Nacho and Don Ramon in private. When they had all gathered, Don Juan said: "The people of my village and all the region around want me to thank you for what you have done for us. We appreciated the medicine and food you brought at the time of the flood. Then you brought us beans to plant and now we have food for our families until the next crops are in.

"The medicine and clothes we accept with profound gratitude, but the beans we want to pay back. Each man brought back the amount of beans he took to plant, and we sold them at the present market price." He opened his satchel and counted out the money in small bills and change.

When Jim said it wasn't necessary for them to pay for the beans he said: "You know, Doctor, it isn't good for a man to receive too much charity. It does something to his dignity. Therefore, you must accept this. You helped us in our desperate times, and we will always be grateful."

I wrote to the person who had sent the money, and asked if we could use the money again to help others who needed food and medicine. When we received the answer to use the money, it was set up in a bank as a small loan project. Any man who need- ed a small amount to buy seed or animal to start a new business could borrow money, if the committee of the church approved. The one who borrowed must pay it back in six months, with a small interest. The interest was used as a loan to help someone else for three years, then given back to the borrower. This was their way of each person receiving help, then helping someone else.

And above all each person was told to give thanks to God.

"All the world is God's own field,
Fruit unto His praise to yield;
Wheat and tares together sown,
Unto joy or sorrow grown;
First the blade, and then the ear,
Then the full corn shall appear:
Lord of harvest, grant that we
Whole-some grain and pure may be."

Come, Ye Thankful People, Come, 2nd verse
Henry Alford, 1844

Chapter XV

Mountain Top Experiences

Another wonderful service started in the 1960's when a group of Ophthalmologists came to Ometepec on a working vacation. The first eye-specialist was from Houston, Texas. In one week, he did over fifty eye operations and examined almost a hundred people for glasses. He took the prescriptions to Houston, then sent the glasses back to Mexico with a friend.

The Stewarts, working with the Indians in Xochistlahuaca, had noticed that their adult students had a hard time seeing letters. So Cloyd brought all of them down to have their eyes examined. At the end of the day, the ophthalmologist exclaimed, "All of the Indians are far-sighted. No wonder they have trouble seeing letters. I will send glasses to all of those learning to read, but please explain to them that they need to wear the glasses only when they are reading."

Months later Cloyd told me that a peculiar thing had happened because of those glasses. It was soon learned that knowing how to read was a distinct advantage, and wearing glasses let everyone know you could read. So glasses became a status symbol and soon were worn most of the day.

A month or two after the doctor from Houston was there, a group of doctors from the Christian Medical Society in California wrote us about coming. Jim was still wearing his back brace, and had not been able to work as long hours as he usually did. He was delighted that these doctors were coming and had a long list of patients waiting to see them.

I wrote to them about the condition of the roads, and the bridges being out. The Ometepec airport was still not in very good condition and plane flights very irregular, if at all. They were to arrive in Acapulco in time to catch the early plane to Ometepec.

On the day they were to come, it was raining again and we wondered what they would do. Jim had thought of flying over to meet them but the rain stopped him also. We had no way to reach them by telegram, so had no way to know what to plan.

I sent a telegram to a friend in Acapulco to see if he could find Dr.Robb Hicks and his party of ten and help them find a way to come to Ometepec. The friend told me later that he went to all the big hotels in Acapulco, found four Doctor groups but none directed by Dr. Robb Hicks going to Ometepec.

At supper that night, the girls staying with us wanted to know if they should make the beds for the visitors. They were to have exams at school the next day and I knew they wanted to study. "No, you don't need to tonight," I said. "Those folks might not even get here tomorrow, so you can study tonight and make the beds after the exams tomorrow, if they get here."

I helped Jim take his back brace off and get ready for bed. He was always so calm. Sometimes it really made me furious that he could be so calm when I was very worried about someone or some thing.

Jim reached into the drawer of his bedside table and handed me a pill. I recognized it as a sleeping pill Dr. Yanez had given him when he first broke his back. "Take this," he said, "get a good night's sleep. You have worked too hard today getting ready for these people and you don't need to worry all night about them. They are seasoned travelers and old enough to figure things out for themselves. The sun will shine tomorrow."

At ten o'clock I took the sleeping pill and lay down for a good night's sleep. At ten thirty, just as I was beginning to get sleepy, the night watchman knocked on the window. "Senora," he called, "there is a whole truck load of doctors at the gate. Where am I to put them!"

"Open the gate and let them on the back porch," I called, "I'll be there as soon as I get dressed."

Jim was already asleep, but was wide awake when he heard the night watchman. "Help me with my brace before you take off," he said. "I'll be there in a minute or two."

A cargo truck was backed up to the porch door and our

visitors were already unloading their bags and baggage. Lenore, wife of Dr. Hicks, was the only woman of the group. They were wet, tired, hungry, but laughing about their trip.

"How in the world did you get here?" I asked.

"The hard way," one of the men exclaimed.

"When we landed in Acapulco, they told us there would be no flight to Ometepec until next week. We saw no red-headed Jim Boyce, so figured he couldn't fly either. At the airport a taxi driver said a bus would be leaving at one o'clock and if we wanted to go by bus he would take us to the bus station."

"What we didn't understand was that we would have to change buses at every river, crossing the river in dug-outs."

When they reached the last river before climbing up to Ome-tepec, there was no bus to meet them. It was now almost ten o'clock at night, it was raining, and they were standing on the very wet river's edge. A truck driver was waiting to take cargo to Ometepec and offered to take them to the hospital if they could ride standing up.

"Have you had anything to eat? " I asked. I often bought tor-tillas at the riverside stand at this place, but knew they would not be making any at this hour of the night.

The doctor's wife spoke up. " We had breakfast on the plane from California. Didn't have time to eat at the airport, and were afraid to eat what was offered us at the river crossings. I, for one, am starving!"

I was thankful for eggs, sweet rolls, refried beans, and instant coffee. By this time, I was feeling that sleeping pill and I still had to make beds. I excused myself and left the visitors eat-ing. I was soon joined by Lenore, who said she was a nurse and knew very well how to make beds. Rather than having her think I was plain drunk, I told her about taking the sleeping pill. "You know," I said, "these beds come up to meet me every time I throw a sheet over them. I hope I can stay awake until I finish making them."

My new friend thought my confession was hilarious. She helped me make the beds, then went to tell the men why I had to go to bed. The next morning the sun was shining, the hospital buzzing with activity and I felt fine.

Dr. Jerre Freeman, an ophthalmologist from Memphis, Tennessee, came with his family, and some other doctors, for Thanksgiving week. He examined many eyes and did numerous cataract surgeries. As in other times we had visiting doctors, the people gather from miles around for his consultations. Dr. Freeman has returned every Thanksgiving week since that first visit and people are always waiting for him. There are no more radio announcements about the visits for everyone knows the doctors who can make blind people see will be there the fourth week in November.

Over the years, we had several laboratory technicians. Some stayed a year, some a month or two, some just for a working vacation. Then came a retired Public Health nurse from St. Louis, Missouri, Miss Virginia Pipe. She didn't look a day over forty, and was full of energy, enthusiastic, cheerful and a beaming Christian. She didn't know much Spanish, but knew how to laugh at herself when she made a mistake.

Virginia had driven to Ometepec in a Volkswagen, nevertheless we didn't like for her to drive out to Acapulco by herself. Usually, there was someone very glad to go with her. Twice she asked me to go with her to help buy some lab equipment. On the first trip when we reached the river we saw a long line of trucks waiting to cross on the barge. "Oh, Marguerite," Virginia moaned, "if we have to wait for all of these to pass first, we won't get to Acapulco until after the stores close."

We watched the barge unload. After the trucks came a small car. "Virginia," I asked, "can you drive this car into a tight place behind one of the trucks?"

"I've driven in much tighter places than that," she laughed.

I walked past all the trucks and approached the man in charge.

"Senor," I asked, "If you will permit, my friend in the small Volkswagen would like permission to go across behind the trucks on the next barge."

"Tell her to drive up here and park over on that side," he replied, pointing to a small parking place out of the way of the on-coming trucks.

As we drove past the parked, waiting trucks, many of the men shouted at us in a joking way. Some blew their horns and whistled. "Just smile and wave a `thank you'," I said to Virginia.

"What are they saying?"she asked.

"I don't think I can translate it for you," I said, remembering Johnny and his introduction to obscenities. "Just smile and take it as a joke."

One trucker standing near the front line, said to the man in charge,"Let them go on the next barge. They are from the hospital in Ometepec, I know them."

Virginia did a beautiful job of driving that little bug into a very tight place on the next trip of the barge, and we gave the man in charge a tip so he would remember us when we returned.

On the next trip with Virginia, there was a temporary bridge over the river so we didn't have to wait. However, about a mile down the road we had a flat tire. "Marguerite, do you know how to change a tire?" she exclaimed.

"Where is your jack?" I asked. I knew very little about changing a tire, but I knew that was the first thing needed.

"I don't even know if I have one," Virginia replied.

We heard a vehicle coming up the hill from the river, and I told Virginia to act as if we knew what we were doing. Around the curve came a rusty, windowless, beat-up jalopy filled to total capacity with young teenagers. They whooped and hollered, laughed and whistled as they passed and disappeared around the next curve.

In a short time we heard them returning. The boys jumped out before the driver made a complete stop.

"Dona Margarita," one of them greeted me, "can we help you? We couldn't stop when we recognized you because this junk we are riding needs plenty of space to stop or turn around."

"We don't have a jack," I moaned, "Do you have one that will fit this car?"

The other boys had been looking over the Volkswagen and admiring its beauty and size.

One of the boys heard my question and there was more loud laughing. "A jack? Senora, we have four wheels and a motor that sometimes runs. When something happens we just leave it and walk."

Before we knew what was happening, the boys gathered around the back end of the car and lifted it up while two of them changed the tires. In just minutes, we were ready to go again.

I offered to buy them a tank of gas, and they declined. "Oh, no," the leader said, "This junk wouldn't know how to run with its tank full." They waved and whistled as we started on toward Acapulco.

"God sends His angels in rusty, old jalopies sometimes, doesn't He?" Virginia said, "Did you know them? They certainly knew who you were."

"I can't remember his name, but the one who called me by name was a player on the high school soccer team last year. They went up in the mountains to play another school. Coming back, they had a wreck. The truck turned over and the injured were brought to the hospital. They were all so sweaty, bloody and covered with dust we could not tell one from the other."

"One boy had lost quite a bit of blood and was the most seriously hurt. Jim sent for his parents to see if one of them would give blood. Getting someone to give blood has always been a problem here. They have a fear of losing blood for some reason.

"While we were waiting, one of the players from our church came to me and said, `Dona Margarita, if my blood is the right type I will give it. If Jesus gave all of His for me, surely I can give a little for my friend.' After he offered, several others also offered, but I told them to wait. Most of them had some kind of injury, and I didn't know how badly hurt anyone was."

The injured boy's father soon came, however, and was ready to give blood. Not one life was lost, but it was quite awhile before they played soccer again.

Virginia and I were both very thankful that day for God sending help to us. We would never have fixed that tire with our knowledge or skill.

One morning about a week after Virginia returned from Acapulco, Don Ramon came striding into the office. The look on his face told me immediately that he had some other great idea to present. It didn't take him long to start telling me about it.

"Dona Margarita, you realize, don't you, that in June the hospital will be ten years old? Also this June the Presbytery plans to ordain Nacho and install him as pastor of this church. So why don't we have both of these occasions the same weekend and invite everyone? On Saturday we can have a ceremony for the hospital, with a barbecue here in your yard. Then on Sunday we can have a beautiful service at the church and have a dinner for all who attend in the church patio."

"That's a brilliant idea!" I exclaimed. "What do we do first?"

"You talk to the Doctor about it and I'll talk to Nacho when he comes this week-end. You talk to Dr. Yanez also and the nurses, and I'll tell the officers at the church. They will be all for it, for they have already started talking about a banquet for Nacho when he is ordained. You and the doctor make a list of who should be invited to the hospital anniversary, and the officers, with Nacho's help, will make a list for the Sunday service."

I saw that he and the church officials had already discussed this whole idea, and were pleased they had thought about including the hospital in the great occasion.

That night when I told Jim about the plans, he was delighted. "If Don Ramon is in charge, I won't have to worry about it, so I say go ahead. I know several I'd like to invite to be speaker on Saturday, but let me think it over a day or too."

"We'll need music," I said. "Why don't we ask for the best: The Choir of the School of Sacred Music in Mexico City."

"You do aim high," Jim laughed, "but try it. They just might like to come see a part of Mexico that few have seen."

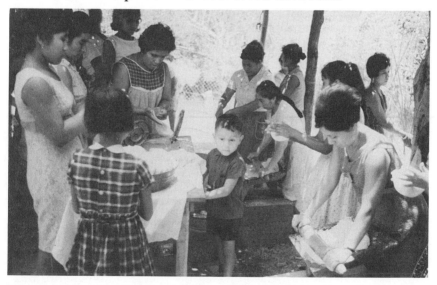

Women of the church preparing dinner for celebration of Nacho's ordination.

Nacho and Maria were also brought into the plans and we were all surprised at the enthusiasm everyone showed for the occasion.

The goats were fat in 1978 and corn plentiful and the congregations in the mountains and coastal plains promised enough food for both days. After the awful floods of the year before, the fields had been fertilized by the top soil washed down from the mountains, and all the wells were full, so there was water for plants and animals.

People who had no land offered to help clean and fix up the church and many women came to the hospital to set up their "comals" (a large flat clay vessel to cook tortillas).

The two days chosen for the fiesta were beautiful. The visitors from the United States included our good friend, Rev. Thomas Currie, Jr., from the Oak Cliff Church in Dallas. The Presbytery sent a commission to ordain Nacho, and they,too, had a part in the hospital celebration. Several choirs came to sing, including the Choir of the School of Sacred Music.

There was just one thing more needed: a piano in the hospital. I had wondered about that but never dreamed we could move our old, heavy upright piano from our house over to the hospital. However, I underestimated the determination of the church people to have this a perfect celebration. Several of the young men came to me and said they could move the piano, if I would give them permission to tie two long poles on it. I gave them permission but still had my doubts about their plans.

The visiting musicians and I stood by in awe as the men tied one long pole to the front of the piano, and another to the back. Then carefully, three men on each end lifted the poles onto their shoulders. "Vamanos," (Let's go), the leader shouted. With the piano about two feet off the ground, the men carefully marched over to the hospital and set the piano down.

"Unbelievable," our visitors exclaimed and I joined in. (I must admit, however, I was even more impressed that night when they repeated the process and sat the piano down again in our living room.)

Everything went off beautifully on Saturday. Neither Dr. Boyce nor Dr. Yanez was called to deliver a baby until after the dinner. The music was beautiful, and even though the program

Crowd arriving for tenth anniversary of hospital.

was long according to some of us, it was not too long for the majority present.

Sunday was another beautiful occasion. Jim and I were as proud of Nacho as his own family. The small church building was crowded, the porch full, and the patio filled to capacity with people standing. Fifty-two elders and ministers from both Mexico and the United States took part in the ordination service.

Our cups were truly running over as we saw Nacho, one of the first fruits of those early days in Ometepec, ordained as the Pastor of the "Iglesia Presbiteriana Fe y Luz" (Faith and Light Presbyterian Church.)

Early the next morning, our visitors began to leave. There were flights to Acapulco, Oaxaca, and Mexico City that morning and each flight carried some of our visitors back to their work. Again, we came down off a mountain top experience to the valleys where the sick were waiting.

Several of the people who came in from around Ometepec to the celebration stayed to see the doctors. They needed medicine to take home, and some wanted to discuss their ills. A number who were on long term treatment for tuberculosis or leprosy, the doctor had told to remain for a good check-up.

By 1968, Jim had almost a hundred leprosy patients in his file.

He had been reporting these cases to the National Public Health Department through the years, but never had a response from the department. Then one morning a young doctor representing the division of Public Health in charge of Leprosy in Mexico, came to the hospital. He had been sent to check on the cases reported by Jim, and wondered if he could see the files on the patients, and maybe a case or two of Leprosy. Jim was more than glad to let him see the files, and offered to fly him to some of the villages or ranches to see the patients. They saw several patients, and the young doctor was impressed with the gratitude these patients expressed for Jim.

He told Jim that in Mexico City they had no cases of leprosy on the books for this entire region. Therefore, they were surprised at the number of cases that had been found by this one Dr. Boyce. Jim then told the young visiting doctor about the custom of the region of demanding that the family of a leper deal with the problem by making the sick one "disappear."

"You won't find them in the cities and towns," Jim said. "They are still hidden on the ranches, where their families protect them from outsiders."

The young man from Mexico City was impressed with the living conditions of the region, and with the hospital being located in such an isolated town.

"We're not so isolated now," Jim remarked, "With the new road coming in, we are beginning to see many changes. Some changes are good, some not so good, but education is getting better. Now nationally trained teachers are more and more willing to come to this region to live."

The young doctor must have made a good report when he returned, for shortly afterward Jim received a letter from the head of the department thanking him for the good work he was doing in this region. He congratulated him on the hospital, and expressed his appreciation for his records of the patients. He also said his department would furnish medicine for all the leprosy patients and we would not have to order medicine from London.

One day in late August of 1968, the large passenger bus pulled a half block off its route to let a woman and small child off. We knew it must be an emergency, for usually people walked from the corner. It was very hard to turn a large bus around on this side street, but the drivers were kind men, and when they saw a person too sick to walk, they would drive up to the door. This woman had one leg bandaged and was pulling herself along with a stick as a crutch. She was very thin and obviously in great pain. The little girl opened the door and helped her mother hop to a chair.

The nurse on duty saw the woman almost fall over and rushed to help her to the examining room. She went to call the Doctor from one of the patient rooms. "Ay, Doctor, we have a bad case in the examining room. The odor is terrible. It's a broken leg, exposed bone, but it has been broken for a long time."

When Jim entered the room, the woman untied a large bandanna and held it out to the doctor. "It's all the money I have, Doctor. Is it enough for you to do something for my leg?"

"The money is enough," Jim said. Then after looking at the leg he added, "But there is nothing I can do for your leg but amputate, and the sooner the better."

"I know that," the woman said, "That's what the Doctor in Pinotepa National said you would have to do. He couldn't because he doesn't have the instruments. He told me that you are the only one in the region who can help me. Please do whatever you need to do, for I am so tired of this awful pain."

Jim turned to the nurse and told her to take the woman's history and he would call Paula to set up for surgery. He would finish making rounds, then operate on the woman.

The little girl sat by her mother's bed while the nurse asked questions. The child, Minerva, answered many questions because her mother was so weak. The two of them had been in the field clearing to plant when the mother stepped in a hole and her leg cracked like a big stick. "Lots of blood came out," Minerva said. "It was very bad. I ran to get my step-grandmother and some neighbors helped us get my mother back to the house. They all said the leg was very bad and my mother would have to go to see a doctor. But the nearest doctor was a long way away, and we didn't have a donkey, so we had to walk."

Minerva, a seven-year-old child was told to help her mother along. They made a stick for a crutch and bandaged the leg with rags. All anyone had for pain was aspirin. Whenever they would come to a house, Minerva would beg for food or money. The food they would eat, the money was tied in the bandanna to pay the doctor. They couldn't go very fast, and soon the mother had fever. When they would come to a stream of water the mother would sit in it until the fever went down. Minerva would wash their clothes and dry them on a bush. It took them a number of weeks to reach Pinotepa National, Oaxaca, a town about fifty kilometers from Ometepec.

There they found a doctor, but he said they had to come to Ometepec. Minerva had helped her mother sit under the shade of a tree on the zocalo, (town square), and then she began begging in all the stores and stands within sight of her mother. She watched the buses come into town, circle the zocalo and heard the assistant driver call out where they were going. When she heard one call out Ometepec, she hurried behind the bus until it stopped. "Can you take my mother to Ometepec? She has a broken leg and is very sick. The doctor here says she must go to the hospital in Ometepec."

"Where is your mother?" the driver asked.

"Over there under that tree," Minerva told him, pointing to the woman lying down under the tree. She must have looked very sick, for the man turned to Minerva and told her to help her mother to the bus.

"And that's how we got here," Minerva told the nurse. Minerva sat in the ward by her mother's bed during the operation. The evening meal was served, and the nurse on duty gave the child a sweet roll. When she saw how hungrily she ate it, the nurse returned to the kitchen to ask for a glass of milk. The child said "Thank you," but never asked for more.

The next morning after the children staying with us had left for school, Minerva came to my back door. I was sitting drinking my coffee when she asked permission to come in. When I gave her permission, she opened the door and slid into the nearest chair. Folding her hands in her lap she announced, "I have come to stay with you."

"Really? Now why would you want to do that?" I asked.

"My mother will have to stay in the hospital for a long time, and the woman in the next bed told me they won't let children stay in the hospital unless they are sick. And the nurse told me to come see you. She said you had lots of children."

"What about your family back in your town?"

"They don't want me," she said with a sad expression. "You see, my father was killed in another state in an accident in the oil field. So my mother brought me back to her town. Then she married another man, and he was killed in a truck accident. So my mother took me and my baby brother to live with this man's mother. She didn't want me, but my mother said I had to stay and would help her in the fields."

I saw her eyes look at the leftover food on the table. There wasn't much there, but the look on her face told me she was hungry. "Would you like some eggs and chocolate milk?" I asked.

"Oh, yes, thank you," she said, hurrying over to the table.

I scraped the skillet of beans and managed to get a spoonful, scrambled her an egg, and poured up the last of the chocolate milk. She ate everything, then with a smile, thanked me. "Tell your mother that I will talk it over with the Doctor, but, if you stay, you will have to go to school." I said.

"Go to school?" she exclaimed, "You mean I could go to school? I could learn to read? Oh, Senora, how good you are!" She jumped down from the chair and did a little dance around the porch, then came over to me to give me a hug. I was won for life!

Minerva's mother was in the hospital for almost a month. At first, we were all worried that she wouldn't live through the battle she had with infection. Modern medicines and good food worked wonders, though, and after about ten days she was sitting up and smiling. Jim wrote to the National Rehabilitation Hospital and asked if he could send another patient. (He had sent several in years past.) There was a waiting list, but they would accept her as soon as there was an opening.

Minerva went to see her mother every morning as soon as she was awake, then came back to the house for breakfast. She insisted on doing dishes or sweeping, or something to help with the housework. The older girls took her under their care and coached her on how to act at school.

I was amazed at how much one teacher could teach one hundred children. The room was equipped with fifty single desks, but there were two children to the desk. Minerva sat with Eli, the daughter of a women who worked half days for me. The two girls would come rushing in at noon, anxious to show us what they had learned. One day Eli and Bequi came to tell me that Minerva was down at the gate giving away our cookies that had arrived that morning. I looked down at the gate and saw Minerva handing out cookies to a crowd of small children. I waited until she came up to the house with the empty box, then asked her why she had given away our cookies. Her face fell as she realized that she had not asked my permission, "Oh, Senora, I forgot to ask you first. I told some of the girls we were going to have cookies at lunch and they said they had never tasted cookies. And Senora, they were so hungry, and we had so many cookies. You are not mad, are you?"

How could I be mad at this child who had lived most of her life begging? I could understand how she would feel about being able to share now. "No, Minerva, I'm not mad. God wants us to share with those who do not have. But next time please remember to ask me first, for we have many people to feed." I gave her a hug and she went to the hospital to see her mother.

At Christmas, all the children living with us took part in the Christmas program. Minerva was in the children's chorus and loved to sing the songs. One day I was at my desk at home and heard her come in the back door. She was singing about the star appearing in the sky, and waving her stick with a star on the end of it. She suddenly saw me and stopped singing. With a whirl around, holding the star high up, she said, "Oh, Senora, isn't it wonderful that Jesus was born so we can have Christmas?"

"Minerva, how do you celebrate Christmas in your village?" I asked.

Her face fell for a second, then she said, "They don't even know when it is. They don't know about the baby Jesus." Then she smiled and added, "But when I get big I'll go tell them."

The mother was sent to Mexico City, fitted with a prosthesis and taught to walk. She was also given a job working as an extra in a movie studio. The Government had a contract with the movie industry for them to hire as many handicapped people as they could, and Minerva's mother was one of the lucky ones. She returned to Ometepec in the spring to show us how well she could walk and to take Minerva back to Mexico City with her. She promised to send Minerva to school. "The Social Worker said I would have to send her to school, so don't worry about that."

They left for the big city and we lost track of them. But I never lost the love in my heart for that sweet child. I have prayed for her, as I have for all those who passed through our home.

I think when I read that sweet story of old,
When Jesus was here among men,
How He called little children as lambs to His fold:
I should like to have been with them then.

I Think When I Read That Sweet Story of Old
Jemima Luke, 1841

Chapter XVI

"Hasta La Vista"

Long before Nacho was ordained, the members of the congregation were talking about building a church. They heard about numerous lots for sale but most were totally unsatisfactory. Now that Nacho and his family were in residence, the interest in a church building increased, and once more the scouts were out looking.

One day a businessman uptown told Don Ramon that a certain lot just might be for sale. The location was good, so Nacho and Don Ramon went to see the owner of the lot. After discussing many other things, the subject of the lot was brought up. The man said, "Yes, under certain conditions it might be for sale," but they were to tell no one except the church committee. After several weeks, a deal was made and the church had one of the most desirable lots in town. It was on a hillside, but only Main Street was more or less level, so they would plan their building to fit the land.

The plans were drawn by Nacho and the hospital architect. Men, women and children began bringing in rocks from the country side. Families offered to do anything they could: carry material for the masons, clean, dig, whatever could be done by unskilled labor was volunteered by church members.

The walls were made of open cement blocks. This made it possible for the breezes to blow through and keep the sanctuary cooler. It also made expensive glass windows unnecessary. On one corner of the lot, a three room house was built for a manse. The women of the church wanted a kitchen for church socials, and in it they built in the traditional way of making tortillas, and installed a gas stove. Also, they built what most of the women did

not have at home, but wanted very much: they installed a spigot
of water over a sink for washing dishes. In the patio next to the
sanctuary, they built a stage where dramas and programs could
be given. Sunday school rooms were built on a higher level
behind the sanctuary.

For these people it was a tremendous undertaking, but they
were proud of the final product. On January 10, 1971, the building
was dedicated.

Peggi, on her last visit home had told us that her sociology
teacher wanted to come visit us to see how the road affected the
lives of the people. "She is too late," I said laughing. "She should
have come twenty years ago. We are the ones who have seen the
changes from donkeys to airplanes, then to pick-up trucks." Peggi
immediately wanted to know what other changes we had noticed.

"First, notice that we have had many more truck accidents
than gun shots in the last few years. Schools have been built, and
a new secondary school is already too small. Last year one of the
directors of Indian affairs came here to ask me if I knew of an
Indian boy who was finishing elementary school. When I told him
two were finishing that year he told me to send them to him and
he would hire them. The government had recognized that the
Indian children should have schools, but would have to learn
Spanish before age six. So they were starting a pre-school program to teach Spanish, and needed someone who also knew
Amusgo to teach it.

"His offer seemed very good. After teaching two or three
years, the young teachers would be sent to Normal School for one
year free. In the course of a few years, they would receive a feder-
ally recognized teacher's degree."

"Then, of course, you should look in the stores in town for
some of the changes there," I continued, "I guess you were too
young to remember when we first came. There wasn't a light bulb
in a single store in town. Those of us with generators had to buy
the bulbs in Acapulco. Now we're not the only ones in town with
a gas stove. We used to have to send to Acapulco to fill our tanks.
Now they deliver to the door.

"And one of the greatest changes, I think, is the number of
houses that now have built inside bathrooms and installed septic
tanks. Why, just this week, I was at Victor's store and a young boy

came in and asked for a roll of toilet paper. Without thinking at all, the clerk asked, `What color?' Now that's progress!" I laughed and Peggi agreed that was indeed progress.

Jim had come into the room while we were talking and, after we stopped laughing, he added, "And the 'clees,' tell Peggi about my fun with the 'clees.'

"That's your story," I said, "you tell it, I want nothing to do with it."

"It was one of those days when we had worked all day and into the night," he began. "There were three more women in the labor room, and Paula and I were both so tired and sleepy we would take naps between contractions like the women did. Sometimes Paula would call me and sometimes I'd call her. Sometimes the patient would call us both and we would jump to her side.

"About three o'clock in the morning I pushed one tired foot in front of the other down the hall and out the kitchen door of the hospital. The cool air was refreshing and I paused at the gate to take some deep breaths. It was a full moon and there was not a cloud in the sky. I looked up to admire the brightness of the moon. Suddenly I saw a shadow creeping across the face of the moon, and I forgot how tired I was. Pure mischief filled my tired body.

"I called the night watchman who was close by and said, `Look, Don Adolfo, what is that up there on the moon?' He looked up and said, `Why, doctor it's the `clees.' It surely is.'

"Don Adolfo, listen, do you hear anything? This town is quiet. Do you have a bucket you can beat? You and I are going to wake up this town." He looked at me and smiled and I knew I had a companion spirit.

"He was back in a second with two buckets and two sticks. We can't do it here, I said, let's go around to the other side of the house so the noise wont be so loud for the patients."

"Daddy," Peggi exclaimed, "you certainly didn't beat a bucket, did you?"

"Don Adolfo beat the first rhythm and we listened. No answer. So he beat it out again, and we both banged away."

"And I jumped out of bed almost scared out of my wits," I said, "I thought someone was coming right in my window until I heard your father laughing his head off."

"Oh, Don Adolfo and I had a good time that night." Jim said. "One by one, people on the hills around town, began to beat buckets and pans. The dogs were barking, roosters crowing and even a few donkeys braying. I felt totally repaid for all those nights I had been awakened by the `clees' racket."

"Yes, Peggi, the road has made a difference. And so has education. But the greatest difference is shown in the lives of those who have discovered that God loves them, and they have followed His leading in their lives.

"One woman told me the other day that before they started coming to church, her husband made her pull the plow like a donkey. He would beat her, too, to make her do as he wished. Now, she says, he has bought a donkey with the money he used to spend on whiskey, and they sing hymns as they work in the field. I ask you, is there a greater difference than this?"

About this time, the hospital was finally organized under its own Board of Directors and recognized by the Government as a Charity organization. The General Assembly of the National Presbyterian Church was held in Vera Cruz, and Nacho went for the first time as a voting member. We kept their three boys so Maria could go with Nacho.

We had known for several years that our mission board was planning to withdraw all missionaries from Mexico in 1972. The time was getting close and we felt we simply had to go away some place and face some serious questions. Where would we go? When should we leave? How could we ever leave Ometepec and so many people who seemed like family? We were too busy to think straight about it as long as we were on the job.

So the last of June 1971, we drove to Edinburgh, Texas to visit Florence, Dan and our first grandson, born in April. Bill finished his year at Vanderbilt and joined us in Texas. We talked out our problem and circled it from all directions. We prayed again for guidance and direction.

Then one day, as we were back on the circle of when and where, Dan spoke up. "You know, folks, it's not a question of if you are going to leave, it's when you should leave. Look at it from that perspective and consider several things. The new Board of Directors of the hospital is already named. Edson is going to Ometepec this summer to help the new administrator in the change over. Dr. Yanez has been named the Chief of Staff. If you stay, will it cause him any problems in initiating any changes he wants? In one more year, will you be any more ready to leave than you are now?"

We sat quiet for a minute or two, then Jim pushed back his chair. "You are right. If we stay, we might become a problem to them. And I think leaving quickly will be best. I will send telegrams notifying them we are coming back to pack up and will leave in August."

The entire town had heard by the time we returned, and the news spread quickly throughout the region. People came by, begging us to stay. One day a delegation of men representing the Chamber of Commerce and the City Council came and asked to speak to Jim and me privately. They had heard that our Mission Board was calling us home and wanted to know if they could do anything to change their minds. "We'll write letters. We don't want you to leave us. Boyce, we need you," they said to Jim. We thanked them and told them we really didn't want to leave. "However," Jim said, "we are going not just because the mission board says to go, but because we feel it is God's will." It was a hard meeting, and although we truly appreciated what those men were trying to do, it was difficult to explain to them why we felt we had to do it.

I don't think we could have ever gotten through that month without Bill. He climbed up to attic space over the back hall and cleaned out all the treasures the children had put up there when they left for school in the States. We decided to give away or sell most of our furniture. What was left to ship had to be stored in the basement of the hospital.

Most of the decision-making about what to do with furniture, etc. fell on Bill and me. Patients had come in from miles around to see the doctor for the last time. Members of the church congregations in the coastal plains came to bring gifts, and plead with us to come back.

One morning a woman and a little boy came walking into our house calling "Doctor Boyce, Doctor Boyce, I must see you face to face." At first, I didn't recognize Maria, his first leper patient. I had not seen her since her wedding day several years before. She greeted me but insisted she had to see the Doctor.

When Jim walked in, she started crying. "Tell me it's not true. I heard you are leaving Mexico and I have come all the way from Acapulco to hear it from your own mouth. I would not believe any one else. Tell me it's not true."

"Yes, Maria, it's time for me to leave. It is true."

"Then I shall get back on the next bus and never come back to Ometepec. There is no reason for me to come here if you are not going to be here."

The little boy had stood watching us, and Jim looked down at him and asked, "Do you need a good puppy on your ranch? Maria, we have two beautiful little puppies left and if you will allow me to give your son one I would like very much to do so."

"How can I refuse a gift to remember you by?" she cried. "Of course, he can have it."

Jim took the boy by the hand and they went to choose a puppy and have one of the men make a box to carry it back.

Maria and her family lived on a beautiful ranch north of Acapulco, and once a year they invited the youth of the Presbytery to have a week's camp on their ranch. The program was planned by the various church groups and was a highlight in the activities offered for the youth of the churches.

The hospital staff and the church decided to have a farewell banquet for us the night before we were to leave. They worked all day preparing for it, carrying chairs from the church to the hospital, putting up tables down the hall of the hospital, and cooking delicious smelling food in our kitchen. Fortunately, there were no emergency operations that day, and no critically ill patients in the hospital.

At five o'clock, I told the women I simply had to clean up and change clothes before the banquet, and told them not to let anyone else in to see me. I bathed and fell on the bed to rest a few minutes. Jim came rushing in saying he couldn't get away from the people who wanted to talk until he simply walked out.

Bill and some of his friends had packed the car and we were almost ready to leave the next morning. "If we can make it through this night," I said, "maybe we can think straight enough to understand where God wants us to go. Did you ever dream, when we first came here, that it would be so hard to leave?"

The banquet was well planned. The food delicious and the

program good. Some people told funny stories about our first years in Ometepec. We were toasted, we were well-wished, etc., etc. There were tears, and there were laughs.

Then Nacho announced that the last number on the program was a poem written by Tony. He had asked Nacho to read it, but Nacho said he would never make it to the end without crying. So Nacho had asked a visiting minister to read Tony's poem. There were few dry eyes when he finished. In the hushed moment at the end, Nacho led in prayer.

Edson Johnson had come down a few days before to help in the transaction of changing the hospital status, and he remarked on the way to the house, "I have been to many farewell parties, but never to such a tear-jerker. They truly hate to see you leave."

We left very early the next morning, before we would have to say more good-byes. Just the night shift of the hospital and a few patients stood waving to us as we pulled out of the gate. The last words we heard were, "Vaya con Dios. Que Dios les bendiga." (May God go with you. May God bless you.)

My Jesus As Thou Wilt! All shall be well for me,
Each changing future scene, I gladly leave to thee.
Straight to my home above, I travel calmly on,
And sing in life or death, My Lord, Thy will be done.

My Jesus, as Thou Wilt
Benjamin Schmolck, 1704
Trans. by Jane Laure Borthwick, 1854

Mission Accomplished

by Tony M. Estrada
To Dr. J. R. Boyce and family

Dear Friends in Jesus Christ, Our Lord,
I write as one who cannot write
(I scarce can read, how can I write?)
To phrase in simple words that tell,
The love we feel, the esteem we've held
For Dr. Boyce and family.

We gather not to say "Farewell!"
To one we hold in high regard,
It's "till we meet again" instead,
And may your paths be led of God,
The Saviour of the Universe.

To his own land our brother goes,
Back to the soil that gave him birth,
A land he left long years ago,
To live and serve in Mexico.

He never dreamed he'd love her so,
For had he known, would he have left
To sail to distant, foreign shores
Or known the traveler's homeward call?

But now your mission is complete,
The parting come—postponement gone,
And still we say, "Remain awhile."
For we are "family";this is "home."

Your name will now be "Shepherd," for
Throughout the years the wounded sheep
Have found a refuge in the fold
Called "Friendship Home" a place of peace.

"Protector of the Weak" you're called
In memory's hall, the wounds of
Thousands have been healed, God's grace
Flowed through your hands and stood off death.

Elect of God, your kindly deeds
Of mercy done to rich and poor
Will leave a trailing legacy of love
In Christ's own Holy Name.

And now that you are homeward bound
To live among your own, recall
These simple words that fly, like birds,
Leaving the nest to winter's cold.

We cannot fail the Gospel's truth,
Deep-planted in our soil, but please
Come to us once again, dear friend,
For we can never say "Farewell."

Translated by Dr. James Hervey Ross.

Epilogue

Coming back to the States at age fifty-six and not even knowing where we were going seemed foolish to some people, and was rather traumatic for us. However, we felt it was the right thing to do and that God would guide us. With two children in college and two in graduate schools, Jim also had to return to school to pass examinations in order to get his license to practice in the United States.

That was the year we learned what being in debt meant. Also we were shown again in the next few years how wonderful God is in opening doors and supplying our needs. With the help of Christian doctors, Jim was offered several jobs where he could work part time and have time to study. There were three examinations given six months apart. The first was required of all graduates of foreign medical schools. That was obligatory before even applying to take the other two. We spent the winter of 1971 in Florida where Jim joined several other foreign medical graduates in the University of Miami for special courses in preparation for the "big" exam. In the spring of 1973 he took his last exam and received a call to come to East Tennessee.

Jim was very busy from the first day in Athens and seldom had time to fly his plane. He made several trips to speak on missions, but did not need to fly as he had in Mexico. The plane also needed to be "Americanized"—more instruments, a hanger fee and regular repairs from the years of being in the tropics. Several people offered to buy "The Messenger II," but Jim said he wanted that special plane to be used in some special way for the Lord's work. One day Jim received a call from a man in the northeast corner of our state. He had heard that there was a Piper Cub in

Athens that might be for sale. He wanted to buy just such a plane for the use of training missionaries to fly.

Could we have asked for a better use of the Green Stamp plane? It was now over ten years old but was in good condition. We were assured it would be the perfect plane for training young missionaries to fly in rugged conditions on the mission fields. (This we already knew from experience!) We hated to part with that very special plane, but knew in our hearts that everyone who gave those green stamps would be glad to know it was still working to spread the Good News of Jesus throughout the world.

In the fall of 1982, we had another traumatic turn in our lives.

Ometepec Market—1983; Except for the new building in the background it looks the same as in 1952.

We received a call from Mexico saying that Ometepec had had a very bad earthquake and could we come help? The hospital had been so badly damaged it had to be closed. Some 80 per cent of the houses in town had been declared hazardous for living. We took a vacation and went to see for ourselves what we could do.

We were met in Mexico City by Nacho and his family, Lupe and her two boys, and Chavela and one of her daughters. They quickly carried our bags to their three cars and drove through that Mexico City traffic as if they had lived there all their lives. We went to Chavela's house where we had dinner and talked for hours.

About three years after we left Mexico, Nacho had been called to one of the largest Presbyterian Churches in Mexico City. He had already served a two year term as Moderator of the National Presbyterian Church. (He was to serve another two year term in the late 1980s.) Chavela's husband had died and left her a drug store to run to support their two girls. The girls were students in the National University of Mexico in the City. Lupe was a Director of Nurses in one of the large hospitals and also busy writing study books for nurses training. Her two boys were younger but doing well in school. Nacho's three boys were in the University. All of the young people were active in the Youth programs in the Prince of Peace Presbyterian Church where Nacho was pastor.

In Ometepec we saw the damage the earthquake had done, and once again our hearts cried out for the people in this place we so dearly loved. We didn't stay long but we saw enough to know we would work to raise some money to help rebuild the hospital.It was still (and is today) the only hospital within a 100 mile radius that is open 24 hours a day.

After our trip to Mexico, we could not forget the sights we had seen nor the pleas for help. Earlier that year we had heard that the building where Jim had his office was to be torn down and a new medical building was being built to accommodate all the doctors in this building and several new doctors who were to settle in Athens.

So I was not surprised one morning to hear Jim take a deep breath and propose a new direction in our lives.

"Honey," he began, "I'll be sixty-nine on my next birthday. We've paid off our debts. Our children are through school. What would you think of retiring and going back to Mexico to help them repair the hospital?" Of course! What else could we do?

In the fall of 1983, the hospital was reopened and celebrated its twenty-fifth anniversary. The Governor sent his representative. The State Medical Society sent a delegation, and local Medical Societies from all up and down the coast were on hand. The National Presbyterian Church sent its Moderator, and Nacho and Maria were also there to take part on the program. Chavela and

Lupe with their children drove down from Mexico City, and many of the children who had been a part of our lives returned as grown men and women, leaders in church and society. Truly our cup was overflowing.

Throughout all the years our own children were very supportive. We had told them all that we would never be able to leave them any money, but we would help them get a good education in the field of their choice.

Jimmy has been in teaching and research since receiving his PhD in Physics. He works for C.E.B.A.F. in New Port News, Va., is married to Linda Neal, a specialist in Libraries for Children. They have two children, Patricia and Neal.

Florence is a bi-lingual teacher with the Texas Educational Agency. Dan is on the staff at Austin Presbyterian Seminary. Their two boys, David and Peter both attend the University of Texas in Austin.

Peggi is a Presbyterian Minister doing mission work in Hollister, Idaho, and Jackpot, Nevada. She is working with seven denominations to organize the Jackpot Community Christian Church. About half of Jackpot are Latin Americans so Peggi's Spanish is a great benefit.

Elizabeth, our dedicated musician, was killed in an automobile accident in 1973 in Dallas, Texas.

Bill is in Huntsville, Alabama working for Boeing Aerospace Company. He has degrees in Public Health and is interested in the health of astronauts in space. He is married to Karen Falk, and they have two children, Carolyn and Billy.

For several years after returning to the U.S., we lost contact with the Wood boys, but the three older ones have renewed correspondence since finishing school. Kenton is a missionary in Acapulco, working with Nacho to organize and build churches. He is married and has four children.

Van is doing mission work in Southern California, is married and has four daughters.

Timothy is a missionary pilot in South America, presently living in Bogota, Columbia. He is married and has three boys.

Daniel and Benjamin are both in business in California.

Praise God from whom all blessings flow.
Praise Him all Creatures here below,
Praise Him above ye Heavenly Host,
Praise Father, Son and Holy Ghost.